Study Guide

for

UNDERSTANDING CRIMINAL JUSTICE

STEPHEN C. LIGHT
SUNY at Plattsburgh

West/Wadsworth
I(T)P® An International Thomson Publishing Company

Belmont, CA • Albany, NY • Boston • Cincinnati • Johannesburg • London • Madrid • Melbourne
Mexico City • New York • Pacific Grove, CA • Scottsdale, AZ • Singapore • Tokyo • Toronto

TABLE OF CONTENTS

CHAPTER ONE
AMERICAN CRIMINAL JUSTICE: AN OVERVIEW

Learning Objectives

After completing this chapter, you should understand the following topics:

1. The agencies that form the structure of American criminal justice, and how they address the tasks of legislation, policing, adjudication, and punishment.

2. Typical stages of the criminal justice process, from reporting of a crime to administration of the sentence.

3. How misdemeanor crimes and juvenile offenses are treated differently from adult felony offenses.

4. What it means to say that we will study criminal justice scientifically, and why the scientific approach is important. How the consensus and conflict perspectives can help to guide our thinking about these issues.

5. Key problems faced by American criminal justice.

6. Models of the criminal justice process, and criticisms of them.

7. How peoples' position on the ideological spectrum relates to their preferred methods of controlling crime.

Chapter Summary

1. Criminal justice is society's response to crime, as embodied largely in the workings of criminal justice agencies--police, courts, probation, parole, correctional, and juvenile justice agencies. A great deal of crime control activity and disorder management is non-governmental. These efforts include private security, privately managed correctional facilities, and citizen crime control.

2. The structure of governmental criminal justice is made up of organizations involved in legislation, policing, adjudication, and punishment. The process of criminal justice consists of a set of steps through which criminal suspects must pass. Few defendants proceed through all stages.

3. American criminal justice is beset by problems that include fragmentation, large size, high costs, court backlogs, prison/jail crowding, and lack of agreement on goals and methods.

4.   The study of criminal justice follows the scientific method, making use of theory and research. Consensus theory and conflict theory help to guide our thinking about society's response to crime.

5.   Some critics feel that the process model is inaccurate. Alternative views of criminal justice are offered by the crime control and due process models. Other models include the family model, the social learning model, the human rights model, the rehabilitation model, the justice model, the loose coupling model, the funnel model, and the radical model.

6.   Crime is a moral and political issue. Crime control policies are heavily influenced by liberal and conservative ideological positions.

Chapter Outline

Introduction

The **Running Story in the Part 1 Opener** details the case of Dawn Hamilton, a young girl who was murdered. Further installments in the running story appear in the openers to Parts 2, 3, and 4 of the book. The running story illustrates the stages of the criminal justice process, and some of the issues and ambiguities surrounding criminal justice in America.

A.   **Criminal justice** is society's response to crime.

B.   The **structure** of criminal justice is its framework of offices, institutions, and organizations.

C.   The **process** of criminal justice consists of a series of steps through which criminal suspects must pass.

I.   The Structure of American Criminal Justice

A.   **Legislation** is the making of laws by the U. S. Congress and state legislatures. Legislation is a key component of criminal justice.

B.   **Policing** involves the tasks of law enforcement, order maintenance, and service. Policing is carried out by public and private police.

C.   **Adjudication** is the process by which courts arrive at decisions in particular cases.

D.   **Punishment** is administered in prisons, jails, and probation/parole agencies, which are collectively referred to as the **corrections** component of criminal justice.

E.   **Non-governmental social control** is crime control by persons and groups outside of government.

    1.   **Private security** officers are employed by individuals and organizations.

    2.   **Privately managed correctional facilities** strive to save money on construction and operating costs.

    3.   **Citizen crime control** efforts are undertaken by individuals and community groups to prevent crimes from occurring.

II.   *The Criminal justice Process* is a series of steps that criminal suspects must pass through. Not all suspects pass through every step, however. Steps in the criminal justice process include:

A.   **Reporting of the crime** by citizens. A great number of crimes are never reported to the police.

B.   **Pre-arrest investigation** by police officers.

C.   **Arrest** of suspects by taking them into custody. Arrests must be based on probable cause.

D.   **Booking** - administrative processing of suspects after arrest.

E.   **Post-arrest investigation**, in which the police continue to gather evidence. Suspects may be interrogated, or required to participate in a lineup or showup.

F.   The **decision to charge**, which is made by the prosecutor.

G.   **Filing of the complaint**, which is a document that states the charges.

H.   **Review of the complaint by a magistrate**, to ensure that arrest is based on probable cause.

I.   **Initial appearance and bail decision**.

J.   **Preliminary hearing**, in which a judge decides whether there is sufficient evidence to support continued prosecution of the suspect.

K.   **Grand Jury review**, in which a panel of citizens decides whether the evidence supports prosecution. If so, an indictment is prepared.

L.   **Filing of indictment or prosecutor's information**, which are formal statements of the charges, in preparation for trial.

M.   At **arraignment**, the charges are read to the defendant, who enters a plea.

N.   **Pretrial procedures** determine which evidence may be admitted at trial.

O.   At the **trial**, the jury decides whether the defendant is guilty of the charges, or not guilty.

P.   **Sentencing**

Q.   **Appeals and Collateral Challenges,** in which the trial record in reviewed by an appeals court.

R.   **Administration of the sentence**

S.   The **misdemeanor process** is similar to the felony prosecution process, but much more simplified. Defendants can request a trial, but most plead guilty (often by mail).

T.   Young persons who violate the law are dealt with by the **juvenile justice** process, which assumes that young persons are not fully capable of criminal responsibility. In certain cases, juveniles may be prosecuted in the adult criminal justice system.

III.   *Approaches to Criminal Justice*

A.   The **scientific approach** requires us to be objective--to hold our biases aside. It involves using empirical research to test theories. **Consensus theory** assumes normative consensus. It asks how criminal justice agencies contribute to social order. **Conflict theory** assumes a struggle between groups with varying levels of power. It asks who benefits from existing criminal justice arrangements.

B.   Current **criminal justice problems** include

        1.   The **fragmented nature** of criminal justice. Thousands of agencies nationwide.

        2.   **Large size and high cost** ($105 billion annually).

        3.   **Court backlogs and prison/jail crowding**. Leads to "assembly-line justice."

        4.   **Disagreement over goals and methods**

C.   **Criticisms of the process model**. Walker's wedding cake model suggests that cases are treated differently, depending on the seriousness of the offense and whether the suspect is well known.

        1.   Crime Control and Due Process Models - Herbert Packer

                a.   **Crime control model** - protection of the public through crime control

                b.   **Due process model** - protection of suspects' rights

        2 .   Other Models - alternatives to the crime control and due process approaches

                a.   **Family model** - criminals should be punished like children are: with love, for their own good.

                b.   **Social learning model** - criminal justice as service

                c.   **Enforcement of human rights** - focus on political, economic, and social conditions associated with crime

                d.   **Rehabilitation model** - treatment of offenders before their return to the community

                e.   **Justice model** - giving offenders the punishments they deserve

                f.   **Criminal justice as loosely coupled** - Political factors cause criminal justice agencies to draw together to work toward a common goal such as drug enforcement

                g.   **Criminal justice as a selection process** - the "funnel."

                h.   **Radical model** - criminal justice is domination of lower class groups by powerful and rich groups

        3.   **Ideology and crime control** - People's preferred methods of crime control are shaped by their ideological positions.

a.   The **ideological spectrum** - radical, liberal, moderate, conservative, reactionary.

b.   The current debate reflects an **age-old debate** between classical criminology and positivism

1.   **Classical criminology** may be traced to Beccaria (1738-1794). Human beings as calculators or rewards/costs, who have free will. Criminal justice should increase costs of criminal behavior. Deterrence as goal.

2.   **Positivism** may be traced to Lombroso (1835-1909). Human behavior is influenced by causes outside of the person, such as poverty, unemployment, and discrimination. Reform of society as goal.

<u>Key Terms</u>

arraignment
arrest
bail
booking
complaint
conflict theory
consensus theory
crime control model
dual court system
due process model
enforcement of human rights model
family model
Grand Jury
indictment
justice model
loose coupling model
post-conviction remedies
preliminary hearing
prosecutor's information
radical model
rehabilitation model
scientific method
selection process (funnel) model

social learning model
wedding cake model
writ of habeas corpus

Critical Thinking Questions

1.   What governmental agencies form the structure of criminal justice in America?

2.   What role do individual citizens, private security, and privately managed correctional facilities play in American criminal justice?

3.   List and briefly describe each of the typical stages of the (felony) criminal justice process.

4.   What is the scientific method? Why is it important to the study of criminal justice?

5.   What some key problems facing American criminal justice today? What do you think can be done about them?

6.   What models have been offered as alternatives to the process model?

7.   How are peoples' positions on the ideological spectrum important in shaping their views of crime and criminal justice?

Selected Readings

Lawrence M. Friedman. Crime and Punishment in American History (New York: Basic Books, 1993). A social history of criminal justice in America, from the 17th Century to the present. Includes a useful chapter on women and criminal justice in the Twentieth Century.

Diana R. Gordon. The Justice Juggernaut: Fighting Street Crime, Controlling Citizens (New Brunswick, NJ: Rutgers University Press, 1990). A critical analysis of U. S. Government "get tough on crime" policies.

Jerold G. Israel, Yale Kamisar, and Wayne R. LaFave, Criminal Procedure and the Constitution: Leading Supreme Court Cases and Introductory Text, (St. Paul, MN: West Publishing Co., 1991). A compilation of items relating to criminal procedure. Offers a general overview and detailed supporting material.

John H. Lindquist, Misdemeanor Crime: Trivial Criminal Pursuit. (Newbury Park, CA: Sage, 1988). An overview of the place of misdemeanor crime in American criminal justice. Includes chapters on sex crimes, victimless crimes, minor property offenses, family violence, pornography, and the situation of victims.

Nancy E. Marion. <u>A History of Federal Crime Control Initiatives, 1960-1993</u> (Westport, CT: Praeger, 1994). Marion traces the evolution of federal crime control policy through the administrations of Presidents Kennedy, Johnson, Nixon, Ford, Carter, Reagan, Bush, and Clinton.

Samuel Walker. <u>Sense and Nonsense about Crime: A Policy Guide</u>, Third Edition (Belmont, CA: Wadsworth, 1994). An examination of liberal and conservative crime-control strategies, in which the author concludes that most crime control strategies are "nonsense."

Sample Test Questions

Multiple Choice Questions

1. The three basic functions of policing are _____, order maintenance, and service.
   a. DARE
   b. law enforcement
   c. determining who is guilty
   -d. legislation

2. _____ are elected law enforcement officials who have jurisdiction at the county level.
   a. state police
   -b. municipal police
   c. marshals
   d. sheriffs

3. Intermediate federal appeals courts are known as _____.
   a. U.S. Justice Courts
   b. U.S. District Courts
   -c. U.S. Circuit Courts of Appeals
   d. Magistrate Courts

4. The "courtroom work group" consists of the prosecutor, the defense attorney, and the _____.
   a. marshal
   -b. arresting officer
   c. jury
   d. judge

5. Which of the following officials bears ultimate responsibility for charging a suspect with a criminal offense?
    a. the arresting officer
    b. the judge
    c. the prosecutor
    d. the appeals court

6. At which stage of the criminal justice process are the charges read to the defendant, who then enters a plea?
    a. arrest
    b. initial appearance
    c. preliminary hearing
    d. arraignment

7. During the process of *voir dire*, prospective jurors who express an inability to sentence a capital defendant to death will be _____.
    a. stricken from the jury pool
    b. allowed to serve, with conditions
    c. allowed to serve, with no conditions
    d. asked to complete a training course

8. The scientific method is based on which of the following precepts?
    a. lack of bias
    b. public dissemination of results
    c. testing theory against real-world data
    d. (all of the above)

9. _____ assumes that criminal justice works to the benefit of all members of society equally.
    a. conflict theory
    b. consensus theory
    c. interactionist theory
    d. (none of the above)

10. _____ assumes that criminal justice is often biased in favor of powerful persons and groups, at the expense of less powerful persons and groups.
    a. conflict theory
    b. consensus theory
    c. interactionist theory
    d. (none of the above)

True/False Questions

T F   11.   At the present time, public police outnumber private police (private security) by approximately three to one.

T F   12.   The type of agency that employs the largest number of police officers in America is county sheriffs.

T F   13.   According to Herbert Packer's crime control model, a primary goal of criminal justice is protecting the public by reducing levels of crime.

T F   14.   The school of thought known as Classical Criminology is most often associated with the ideas of Emile Durkheim.

T F   15.   It is often said that there is a dual court system in the United States. According to your text, there are actually 51 separate court structures in the U.S.

Essay Questions

16.   American criminal justice addresses the four key tasks of legislation, policing, adjudication, and punishment. Explain what each of these tasks consists of, using specific examples.

17.   The structure of criminal justice consists of the agencies that carry out the duties of criminal justice on a daily basis. What are these agencies?

18.   The process of criminal justice involves a series of steps that criminal offenders typically pass through. Discuss each of these steps.

19.   The conflict and consensus approaches provide useful models for guiding our thinking about criminal justice issues. What are the primary assumptions of these theoretical perspectives, and what operative questions do they propose we ask about criminal justice?

20.   The debate between classical and positivist explanations of crime hinge of the role played by individuals' free will. Discuss the concept of free will as it applies to these two explanations.

Answers to Sample Test Questions:
1b, 2d, 3c, 4d, 5c, 6d, 7a, 8d, 9b, 10a, 11F, 12F, 13T, 14F, 15T

CHAPTER TWO
CRIME

Learning Objectives

After completing this chapter, you should understand the following topics:

1.   The difference between criminology and criminal justice as fields of study.

2.   How the concept of crime may be defined in three ways: as a violation of law, as a social problem, and as a political phenomenon.

3.   The advantages and disadvantages of three methods of measuring crime--police data, victimization data and self-report data.

4.   Types of crime, including violent crime, property crime, public-order crime, white-collar crime, organized crime and political crime.

5.   The major scientific theories of crime, and how they are posed at various levels of analysis.

6.   Why theories of crime are important.

Chapter Summary

1.   The concept of crime may be defined in three ways: as a law violation, as a social problem, and a political classification.

2.   The three principle types of crime data are police data, victimization data, and self reports. Police data include the FBI Uniform Crime Reports (UCR) and the National Incident-Based Reporting System (NIBRS). Victimization data include the National Crime Victimization Survey (NCVS). Self-report studies are usually conducted by individual researchers.

3.   Crime may be divided into six types: violent crime, property crime, public-order crime, white-collar crime, organized crime, and political crime.

4.   The consensus and conflict approaches differ in their implications for how crime are defined, how they are measured, and which types of crime are viewed as most important. The consensus approach assumes that there is little disagreement about these issues, while conflict theory assumes that group struggle plays a key role in how these issues are resolved.

5. Biological theories of crime look for an underlying chemical or physiological condition that causes an individual to commit criminal acts. Modern versions include the XYY hypothesis, the excess-testosterone hypothesis, and the PMS hypothesis.

6. Psychological theories suggest that human behavior is linked to psychological traits. An example is the psychopathic personality hypothesis, which is sometimes ascribed to persons who commit serial murder.

7. Social-psychological explanations locate the causes of crime in the influences of society on individuals' psychological processes. Examples include classical criminology, social control/deterrence theory, and societal reaction or labeling theory.

8. Sociological theories assume that criminal behavior is linked to the structure of society. Influential sociological theories include ecological theory, strain theory, subcultural theory, and conflict theory.

9. Critics argue that a cohesive explanation of criminal behavior does not yet exist. Integrated theory may offer a way of imposing order on the field by combining theories into more powerful explanations. However, not all scholars agree that the integrative approach is appropriate.

Chapter Outline

Introduction

    A.   This chapter examines crime as a social phenomenon, which is the subject matter of **criminology**. Criminologists ask **five key questions**:

        1.   What is crime?

        2.   What are the different types of crime?

        3.   How can crime be accurately measured?

        4.   How much crime is committed?

        5.   What causes individuals and groups to violate the law?

    B.   **Criminal justice** scholars study society's **response to crime**.

I.   *Defining Crime*

    A.   Criminologists define crime in three ways:

1. As a **legal definition** - Crime is behavior that violates the law.

2. As a **social problem** - Crime is a societal condition (such as environmental pollution or poverty) that affects large numbers of people and seems to require some type of solution (consensus theory).

3. As a **political classification** - Crime is a label applied by powerful persons and groups to acts committed primarily by the relatively powerless (conflict theory).

II. *Measuring Crime*

To understand crime, we first must measure it. There are **three types of crime data**:

1. **Police Data**

2. **Victimization Data**

3. **Offender Self-Report Data**

The most important criterion of good data is **validity**, which is the extent to which the data measure what they are intended to measure. Ideally, different measures of crime should agree with one another, which is called **convergence.**

A. **Police Data** are collected by the Federal Bureau of Investigation (FBI) under the Uniform Crime Reports (UCR) program.

1. **FBI index crimes** include murder/nonnegligent manslaughter, forcible rape, robbery, aggravated assault, burglary, larceny, auto theft, and arson.

2. **Advantages of police data**: collected on a nationwide basis, annual reports issued since 1930 allow observation of trends.

3. **Disadvantages of police data**: focus mainly on traditional crimes and tend to ignore other types, are vulnerable to political manipulation, variations in reporting may occur from agency to agency, do not report the **dark figure of crime** which does not come to the attention of the police.

The National Incident-Based Reporting System (NIBRS), begun in 1991, offers improvements over the older Uniform Crime Reports format.

B. **Victimization Data** - The National Crime Survey program began in 1972. Currently known as the **National Crime Victimization Survey (NCVS)**. Based on interviews with a representative sample of the U. S. population aged 12 or older.

1. **Advantages of victimization data**: include crimes that do not come to the attention of the police, and provide a check against police data.

2. **Disadvantages of victimization data** include inaccurate answers to surveys, under representation of the homeless, and underestimation of crimes that do not have a clear beginning and end.

C. **Self-Report Data** - Collected from persons who have committed crimes. Usually gathered by individual researchers instead of the police or other agency. There is no official nationwide self-report program for measuring crime.

1. **Advantage of self-reports**: gives information on people who commit crimes, not just on the crimes themselves.

2. **Disadvantages of self-reports:** Often conducted on small samples that make generalization to larger populations impossible. Subject to errors that plague survey research such as memory lapses and interviewer bias.

III. *Types of Crime*

A. **Violent Crime** is sometimes called **person crime** because it involves a physical attack against a person. Examples include murder, nonnegligent manslaughter, forcible rape, robbery, and aggravated assault. Increased attention has become focused on rape, domestic violence, and hate crime. About 10 million violent crimes occur in the U.S. each year.

Consensus approach - people agree that violent crimes are wrong.
Conflict approach - violent crime as domination of the powerful over the weak

B. **Property Crime** involves taking of property that belongs to someone else. Examples include burglary, larceny/theft, and motor vehicle theft. Annually, there are about 27 million property crimes in the U.S.

Consensus approach - property crime threatens all members of society.
Conflict approach -   the rich and powerful will feel most threatened by property crime.

C. **Public-Order Crime** is also known as **vice crime** because it is thought to violate public standards of morality. Example include gambling, drug abuse and sales, and

14

prostitution. Public-order crimes are sometimes referred to as **victimless crimes** because they may not cause obvious harm to the offender or to society as a whole.

Consensus approach - public-order crime is harmful to society.
Conflict approach - the rich and powerful define acts as public-order crime to protect their interests.

D.   **White-Collar Crime** is committed by people in connection with their employment. **Occupational crime** is committed for personal gain (employee theft, embezzlement, commercial bribery, etc.). **Organizational crime** is committed to further the interests of an organization (false advertising, price fixing, unsafe products, etc.).

Consensus approach - white-collar crime is harmful to society.
Conflict approach - in a capitalist society, there will be a great deal of white-collar crime committed by the rich and powerful.

E.   **Organized Crime** is carried out in an ongoing and systematic manner by a group. It often involves illegal goods and services such as gambling, loan sharking, sale of stolen goods, illegal drugs, prostitution, and pornography.

   1.   The **alien conspiracy model** views organized crime as influenced by groups who have come from outside of the United States, such as the Italian Mafia.

   2.   The **local ethnic groups model** sees organized crime as a loose and shifting network of partnerships entered into for criminal gain.

   3.   The **enterprise model** sees organized crime as similar to legitimate business activity, except that it is conducted in an illegal manner.

F.   **Political Crime** is crime that is related to government. Political crime includes:

   1.   **Crimes against the state**, such as civil disobedience, terrorism, or revolution.

   2.   **Crimes committed by the state** against its citizens, such as corruption, repression of dissident groups, or genocide.

   3.   **International crimes by the state**, which affects victims outside of the United States. Examples include U.S. Central Intelligence Agency (CIA) plots to assassinate foreign leaders.

Consensus approach - crimes against the state are crimes against shared community values.

Conflict approach - political crimes are evidence of conflict between society's interest groups. The government can be an interest group in itself.

IV.   *Causes of Crime*

Explanations (theories) of crime may be organized according to the **level of analysis** at which they are posed. This refers to the basic unit that is being studied, such as the body, the individual person, the small group, or the large group.

A.   **Biological Explanations** assume that crime is caused by a genetic, biochemical, or hormonal characteristic of the human body.

1.   **Physiognomy** - criminal tendencies may be seen in a person's facial features. John Lavater (1741-1801).

2.   **Phrenology** - bumps on people's heads correspond to brain characteristics affecting behavior. Franz Gall (1758-1828) and John Spurzheim (1776-1832).

3.   **Atavism** - criminals are evolutionary throwbacks to an earlier period, and their bodily features resemble humans' ape-like ancestors. Cesare Lombroso (1835-1909).

4.   **Feeblemindedness** - Crime is caused by mental retardation, which runs in certain families. Richard Dugdale, H. H. Goddard.

5.   **Inferiority** - Criminals are physically inferior. Ernest Hooten.

6.   **XYY hypothesis** - males who have an extra Y chromosome will be more violent.

7.   **Excess testosterone hypothesis** - males with elevated levels of male sex hormone will be more aggressive.

8.   **Pre-menstrual syndrome (PMS) hypothesis** - Fluctuations in womens' hormone levels can cause aggressive and criminal behavior.

Biological explanations of crime have been criticized for ignoring how crimes are defined, for adopting stereotyped views of men and women, and for being overly deterministic.

B.   **Psychological Explanations** assume that crime is caused by underlying mental disturbances of individuals, which tend to develop in childhood.

  1.   **Psychiatric-psychoanalytic theories** are based on the work of Sigmund Freud (1856-1839). Crime is due to subconscious mental conflicts and emotional stresses, which can be treated.

  2.   **Personality theories** suggest that peoples' needs, drives, tendencies and motives can affect their behavior.

  3.   **Psychopathic personality hypothesis** - Certain people (psychopaths or sociopaths) are unable to feel guilt or remorse when they harm people. Often invoked to explain serial murder.

Psychological explanations have been criticized for ignoring the influence of political and economic interests in shaping definitions of crime.

C.   **Social-Psychological Explanations** assume that crime results partly from individual factors and partly from group-level influences.

  1.   **Classical Criminology** - people have free will, and they choose to commit crimes if the rewards exceed the costs. Cesare Beccaria (1738-1794).

  2.   **Social Control/Deterrence Theories** assume that all people are motivated to commit crime, but most do not because of inner and outer controls (social control theory) or because the costs outweigh the rewards (deterrence theory, rational choice theory).

    a.   Travis Hirschi's **social bond theory** (attachment, commitment, belief, involvement).

    b.   **Deterrence theory** - Specific deterrence and general deterrence.

    c.   **Rational choice theory** - People make a rational choice to commit crime, after considering a variety of factors.

  3.   **Societal Reaction Theory (Labeling Theory)** - Virtually everyone has engaged in crime on a temporary or experimental basis (**primary deviance**). When people are labeled as criminals, they will be more likely to engage in crime as a career (**secondary deviance**).

D.   **Sociological Explanations** assume that crime is an outgrowth of the ways in which society is organized. Follows from Emile Durkheim's admonition that "Social facts must be explained by other social facts."

    1.   **Strain Theory** - Society produces forces (strains) that push people into crime.

        a.   Robert K. Merton's **anomie theory** - crime is one outcome when society does not provide the means of achieving cultural goals.

        b.   Richard Cloward and Lloyd Ohlin's **differential opportunity theory** - in order to commit crime, people must also have the opportunity to do so.

    2.   **Ecological Theory** - Crime results from rapid social change and urbanization.

        a.   Park and Burgess found that crime was highest in areas of Chicago with the most **social disorganization**, regardless of which groups lived there.

        b.   Shaw and McKay's **cultural transmission theory** suggests that poverty-stricken slum culture perpetuates deviant norms and values.

    3.   **Subcultural Theories** assume that certain groups (subcultures) adopt values and norms in opposition to those of the wider society.

        a.   Sutherland's **differential association theory** - Crime is learned in interaction with persons who hold deviant values and adopt deviant norms.

        b.   Sykes and Matza's **neutralization theory (drift theory)** - People learn to justify criminal acts.

        c.   Walter Miller - Persons who hold to lower class culture exhibit a distinct set of **focal concerns**: trouble, toughness, smartness, excitement, fate, and autonomy.

        d.   Albert K. Cohen's **middle class measuring rod theory** - Delinquency often occurs because lower-class boys fail to measure up to middle class standards at school.

4. **Conflict Theory** - Influenced by the ideas of Karl Marx (1818-1883). Crime is a social definition created by powerful groups to protect their own interests.

    a. Two major approaches within conflict theory.

        1. Crime results from **interest group conflict** . George Vold and Austin Turk.

        2. **Radical conflict theory** - In capitalist society, crime is a label applied by the powerful to the acts of the powerless, in order to protect the interests of the powerful. Richard Quinney.

    b. Two other approaches are outgrowths of conflict theory assumptions.

        1. **Feminist theory** criticizes criminology because it has been dominated by men.

        2. The **African American critique** points out that crime is often related to discrimination against blacks by whites.

E. **New Directions**

    1. **Integrated theories** link the assumptions of two or more theories into a combined approach.

    2. Not all scholars believe that integrated theories are desirable.

Key Terms

biological explanations of crime
classical criminology
conflict theory
criminology
dark figure of crime
ecological theory
National Crime Victimization Survey (NCVS)
National Incident-Based Reporting System (NIBRS)
organized crime
political crime
property crime

psychological theories
public-order crime
self-report data
social problem
strain theories
subcultural theories
Uniform Crime Reports (UCR)
violent crime
white-collar crime

Critical Thinking Questions

1.   Explain what criminology is, and how it differs from the study of criminal justice.

2.   Explain what it means to look at crime as a legal definition, as a social problem, and as a political category.

3.   What are some advantages and disadvantages of measuring crime with police data, victimization data, and self-report data?

4.   Define each of the six types of crime discussed in this chapter, and give an example of each.

5.   How do the implications of the consensus and conflict perspectives differ on how crime is defined, how it is measured, and which types of crime are considered to be most important?

6.   In what ways do the basic assumptions of biological, psychological, social-psychological and sociological explanations of crime differ from each other?

7.   Sociological theories suggest that the way society is organized causes crime. Explain what this means.

Selected Readings and Resources

Bureau of Justice Statistics, <u>Criminal Victimization in the United States</u>, (Washington, D.C.: U.S. Department of Justice, Bureau of Justice Statistics, published annually). A comprehensive report of results from the National Crime Victimization Survey (NCVS). Available in larger libraries or from the Bureau of Justice Statistics Clearinghouse, P.O. Box 179, Annapolis Junction, MD 20701-0179.

William Chambliss, <u>On the Take: From Petty Crooks to Presidents</u>, 2d ed., (Bloomington, IN: Indiana University Press, 1988). A study of organized crime in Seattle, and its links to the wider society and the rest of the world.

Paul K. Clare, <u>Racketeering in Northern Ireland: A New Version of the Patriot Game</u>, (Chicago: University of Illinois at Chicago, Office of International Criminal Justice, 1989). A study of the racketeering activities of paramilitary groups in Northern Ireland, based on in-depth interviews with offenders, police, and community members. Clare concludes that the illegal activities of paramilitary groups are similar to the activities of organized crime syndicates in North America.

Federal Bureau of Investigation, <u>Crime in the United States: Uniform Crime Reports</u>, (Washington, D.C. : U.S. Department of Justice, Federal Bureau of Investigation, published annually). A compilation of official statistics on crimes that come to the attention of the nation's police agencies. Widely available in public and academic libraries.

Mark S. Hamm, <u>American Skinheads: the Criminology and Control of Hate Crime</u>, (Westport, CT: Praeger, 1993). Hamm studies the neo-Nazi youth terrorist phenomenon from a sociological perspective.

Steven F. Messner, Marvin D. Krohn, and Allen E. Liska, <u>Theoretical Integration in the Study of Deviance and Crime: Problems and Prospects</u>, (Albany: State University of New York Press, 1989). A collection of papers that explore the pros and cons of integrated crime theories.

Tony G. Poveda, <u>Rethinking White-Collar Crime</u>, (Westport, CT: Praeger, 1994). Poveda shows how white-collar crime has undermined much of the legitimacy of political and financial institutions in American society.

Nicole Hahn Rafter, <u>Creating Born Criminals</u>, (Urbana, IL: University of Chicago Press, 1997). A fascinating study of how the concept of "born criminal" was created and applied in the late 19th and early 20th centuries.

Joseph F. Sheley, ed. <u>Criminology: A Contemporary Handbook</u>, 2d ed., (Belmont, Ca: Wadsworth, 1995). A comprehensive collection of articles on important topics in criminology.

Sample Test Questions

Multiple Choice Questions

1. Criminal justice is the study of society's response to crime. _____ is the study of crime as a social phenomenon.
   a. Criminology
   b. Victimology
   c. Law enforcement
   d. Criminalistics

2. Official crime statistics include which of the following?
   a. Uniform Crime Reports
   b. National Crime Victimization Survey
   c. Police data
   d. (all of the above)

3. The consensus perspective suggests that the FBI Uniform Crime Reports _____.
   a. are invalid
   b. reflect the crimes that most people consider most serious
   c. reflect the crimes that powerful groups consider to be serious
   d. (a and b only)

4. Vice crime is also known as _____.
   a. public-order crime
   b. political crime
   c. organized crime
   d. white-collar crime

5. Which of the following is an example of a public-order crime?
   a. prostitution
   b. gambling
   c. illegal pornography
   d. (all of the above)

6. Which of the following is an example of a theory of crime that is posed at the biological level?
   a. strain theory
   b. neutralization theory
   c. phrenology
   d. classical criminology

7. Which of the following theoretical approaches assumes that criminal tendencies may be seen in a person's facial features?
    a.   phrenology
    b.   physiognomy
    c.   feeblemindedness
    d.   XYY hypothesis

8. Which of the following is an example of crimes against the state?
    a.   terrorism
    b.   civil disobedience
    c.   revolution
    d.   (all of the above)

9. *Crime is a label applied by the powerful to acts of the powerless.* This statement is closest to the assumptions of which of the following theories of crime?
    a.   radical theory
    b.   consensus theory
    c.   differential association theory
    d.   neutralization theory

10. In order to be considered valid, crime statistics must _____.
    a.   measure what they are intended to measure
    b.   measure reported and unreported crime
    c.   be based on offender self-reports
    d.   be based on interviews

True/False Questions

T F 11. Victimization data include crimes that are not reported to the police.

T F 12. Robbery is usually classified as a violent crime.

T F 13. Occupational crime is committed for the personal gain of the employee.

T F 14. The alien conspiracy model sees organized crime as similar to legitimate business activity, except that it is conducted in an illegal manner.

T F 15. Social-psychological theories of crime assume that crime results partly from individual factors and partly from group-level factors.

Essay Questions

16. Criminologists define crime in three ways: as a law violation, as a social problem, and as a political classification. Discuss the implications of these differing definitions of crime.

17. Discuss the six types of crime, from consensus and conflict points of view.

18. Theories of crime may be posed at biological, social-psychological, and sociological levels. Discuss how theories posed at these levels differ from each other in terms of their basic view of the causes of crime.

19. What methods are used to measure the extent of crime? What are some advantages and disadvantages of each method?

20. What are some sociological theories of crime? What assumptions do they make about how crime is caused? Be specific.

Answers to Sample Test Questions

1a, 2d, 3b, 4a, 5d, 6c, 7b, 8d, 9a, 10a, 11T, 12T, 13F, 14F, 15T

CHAPTER THREE
FOUNDATIONS OF THE CRIMINAL LAW

Learning Objectives

After completing this chapter, students should understand the following topics:

1. The concept of law as a basic social institution.

2. Types of law.

3. How constitutions and the three branches of government create different types of law.

4. Basic assumptions of the natural law, consensus, and conflict models of law.

5. The historical development of legal systems in ancient societies, old England, and colonial America.

6. Types of crimes, and the elements that must be present in order for a crime to have been committed.

7. Defenses that may be offered in support of a plea of not guilty .

Chapter Summary

1. Law is a basic social institution that affects nearly all aspects of society. Scholars disagree over how to define the concept of law, however.

2. Types of law include criminal law, civil law, substantive law, procedural law, constitutional law, case law, statutory law, executive orders, and administrative and regulatory law.

3. The sources of the law are found in constitutions, legislatures, judicial case decisions, and administrative/regulatory agencies. In the judicial branch of the federal government, the Supreme Court plays a uniquely influential role.

4. Natural law theory holds that human conduct is subject to a body of unchanging moral principles. Consensus theory emphasizes the contributions that law makes to social order. Conflict theory sees law as an weapon wielded by the powerful against the powerless. Feminist theory--a variant of conflict theory--points to the ways in which law places women in a disadvantaged position relative to men.

5.   Anglo-American law distinguishes between a number of different types of crimes, including felonies, misdemeanors, *mala in se* and *mala prohibitum* offenses, crimes of moral turpitude, infamous crimes, common law crimes, and statutory crimes.

6.   In order for a crime to occur, *actus reus* and *mens rea* must be simultaneously present, and the defendant's actions must cause the resulting harm.

7.   The notion of criminal responsibility holds that persons cannot be held accountable for their actions if they do not freely and knowingly chose to commit the act, or if they are unaware of the likely effects of their behavior. Persons accused of crimes may present defenses, which are claims that they do not possess criminal responsibility. Typical criminal defenses are age, insanity, mistake, intoxication, duress, entrapment, diminished capacity, necessity, and defense of self or others.

Chapter Outline

Introduction

The warfare in Sarajevo, site of the 1984 Winter Olympic Games, illustrates what can happen when law is weak or nonexistent, or when bitter conflicts arise between groups.

I.   *The Concept of Law*

Scholars disagree over how to define the concept of law. In this book we adopt a social scientific point of view that recognizes 1) the written law and 2) how legal rules are implemented.

A.   **Types of Law**

1.   **Criminal law** specifies permissible and impermissible behaviors, along with punishment to be given to law violators.
   a.   Consensus approach - criminal law meets society's need for formal norms and punishments.
   b.   Conflict approach - criminal law is created by the powerful to benefit the powerful.

2.   **Civil law** governs disputes between individuals.

3.   **Substantive law** defines crimes and criminal sanctions.

4.   **Procedural law** guides criminal justice agencies in prosecution and enforcement of the criminal law.

      B.   **Sources of the Criminal Law**

              1.   **Constitutions** - the basic documents of governments. The Constitution of the United States was adopted in 1787, and the Bill of Rights was added in 1791.

              2.   **Legislatures** create written laws called statutes.

              3.   **The Judiciary**. Decisions of appeals courts create case law.

              4.   **The Executive Branch** of government creates administrative and regulatory law.

II.   *Theories of Law*

      A.   **The Natural Law Model** - The law should be obeyed because it embodies certain timeless moral principles.

      B.   **The Consensus Model** - Influenced by ideas of Emile Durkheim. Law arises from the values, norms, customs, and traditions that are shared by society's people (moral consensus).

              1.   Functions of law
                     a.   social control
                     b.   dispute settlement
                     c.   social change
                     d.   ideological function

      C.   **The Conflict Model** - Influenced by ideas of Karl Marx. Law is created by powerful groups to protect their own interests.

              1.   **Instrumental conflict theory (instrumentalism)** - Society's economic system shapes the other social institutions (including law).

              2.   **Structural conflict theory (structuralism)** - Law is a product not just of the economic sphere, but also the political and ideological spheres.

              3.   **The feminist approach** - Law contributes to the subordination of women by men in patriarchal society.

III.   *History of Legal Systems*

Law arises as societies move from simple forms to more complex ones.

A.   **Law in Ancient Societies**

   1.   **Code of Hammurabi** of Babylon (c. 2100 B.C.) - First example of written law.

   2.   **Biblical Israel** (c. 1200-650 B.C.) - System of law founded on religious principles.

   3.   Athens and the other **Greek City-States** - No body of law separate from religious dictums and ethical traditions.

   4.   **The Roman Empire** (c. 500 B.C. - 500 A.D.) - Law of the Twelve Tables was influential in later centuries. The Justinian Code also influential.

B.   **English Common Law** - Formed by judges from custom and tradition as they decided thousands of cases. Based on precedent (stare decisis - "to stand by a decision").

C.   **History of Law in America** - Colonist brought legal customs and traditions with them from the old country. Influence of English common law through Blackstone's <u>Commentaries on the Laws of England</u>.

IV.   *Law and Crime*

Violations of the criminal law are referred to as crimes.

A.   **Classifications of Crimes**

   1.   **Felonies and Misdemeanors**

      a.   **Felonies** are serious crimes punishable by death or imprisonment for more than one year.

      b.   **Misdemeanors** are less serious offenses which involve imprisonment for less than a year, or no imprisonment at all. Minor misdemeanors are called petty offenses. Some misdemeanors cause a great deal of harm.

   2.   *Mala In Se* and *Mala Prohibitum* **Offenses**

      a.   *Mala in se* **offenses** would be considered wrong even if they were not illegal. Examples include murder, rape, robbery, drug abuse, and arson.

        b.   *Mala prohibitum* offenses are illegal strictly because they have been defined as such by the law. Examples include traffic offenses and fishing without a license.

3.   **Crimes Involving Moral Turpitude** - "Moral turpitude" is hard to define, but it implies baseness, vileness, or dishonesty.

4.   **Infamous Crimes** - The term "infamous crimes" appears in the 5th Amendment. The Supreme Court has defined infamous crimes as those offenses that may result in a prison sentence.

5.   **Common Law versus Statutory offenses**. Common law offenses arise out of customs and traditions, from the English Common Law, and may be unwritten. Statutory offenses are written laws enacted by legislatures.

B.   **Necessary Elements of a Crime**

1.   There can be no crime or punishment **without law**.

2.   *Actus Reus* - "guilty act."

3.   *Mens Rea* - "guilty mind."

4.   *Actus reus* and *mens rea* **must occur together**.

5.   The defendant's actions must have **caused** the crime to occur.

6.   **Harm** must have resulted from the act.

C.   **Criminal Responsibility** - the person must have freely (with free will) **chosen** to commit the act.

D.   **Defenses** are offered by suspects to show that they did not possess criminal responsibility for the act in question. Typical defenses are:

        a.   **Age**

        b.   **Insanity**

        c.   **Diminished responsibility**

        d.   **Mistake**

  e. **Intoxication**

  f. **Duress**

  g. **Necessity**

  h. **Defense of self or others**

Key Terms

actus reus
administrative and regulatory law
case law
civil law
Code of Hammurabi
Common Law
constitutional law
criminal law
executive orders
felony
free will
mala in se offenses
mala prohibitum offenses
mens rea
misdemeanor
natural law model
procedural law
statutory law
strict liability crimes
substantive law

Critical Thinking Questions

1. Why is the concept of law so difficult to define?

2. Discuss the various types of law.

3. What basic assumptions about law are held by the natural law model, consensus theory, conflict theory, and the feminist approach?

4. What functions does the law perform for society as a whole?

5.   How does the criminal law act to protect the powerful at the expense of the powerless, according to conflict theorists?

6.   Do you agree with feminist scholars that the law often acts in the interest of men and against the interests of women? Why or why not?

7.   What are the necessary elements of a crime?

8.   Detail some of the defenses that a criminal defendant may offer in support of a claim of innocence.

Selected Readings

Lawrence M. Friedman, A History of American Law (New York: Simon & Schuster, 1973). Friedman traces the story of American law and the legal profession from the colonial era to the present day.

Thomas J. Gardner and Terry M. Anderson, Criminal Law: Principles and Cases, 5th ed. (St. Paul, MN: West, 1992). A well-written introduction to the substantive criminal law, co-authored by an attorney (Gardner) and a law professor (Anderson). Includes abstracts of important cases.

David Kairys, ed., The Politics of Law, (New York: Pantheon, 1982). A collection of topical articles on law, from a critical perspective.

Charles Warren, A History of the American Bar, (New York: Howard Gertig, 1966). The standard treatment of the rise of the American legal profession.

D. Kelly Weisberg, ed., Feminist Legal Theory: Foundations (Philadelphia: Temple University Press, 1993). Weisberg provides a comprehensive and up-to-date collection of articles on the most important issues in feminist scholarship today.

Sample Test Questions

Multiple Choice Questions

1.   The legislative branch of government influences criminal justice by _____.
    a.   enacting statutes
    b.   deciding which sentences should be applied to which crimes
    c.   allocating funds to criminal justice agencies
    d.   (all of the above)

2. The natural law model states that laws enacted by governments should
   _____.
   a. embody certain timeless moral principles
   b. reflect the will of the majority of citizens
   c. take into account historical changes in social norms
   d. (all of the above)

3. Karl Marx believed that the primary influence on law is _____.
   a. government
   b. the economic structure
   c. religion
   d. norms learned in the family

4. What does the term *stare decisis* mean?
   a. principle
   b. punishment
   c. precedent
   d. prevention

5. The Common Law fleeing felon rule was superseded under United States law by
   the Supreme Court's ruling in _____.
   a. *Tennessee v. Garner*
   b. *Gideon v. Wainwright*
   c. *Miranda v. Arizona*
   d. *In re Gault*

6. A _____ alleges that a defendant did not possess criminal responsibility at
   the time of the crime.
   a. writ of certiorari
   b. defense
   c. cross-examination
   d. guilty plea

7. The defense of _____ alleges that the defendant's mental state at the time of
   the offense makes him or her not guilty of the crime.
   a. insanity
   b. diminished capacity
   c. mistake
   d. duress

8. The 4th Amendment to the Constitution contains which of the following rights?
    a.   right to remain silent
    b.   right to counsel
    c.   right to be free from unreasonable search and seizure
    d.   right to bear arms

9. _____ specifies which acts are permissible and which are not. It defines crimes and criminal sanctions.
    a.   Civil law
    b.   Substantive law
    c.   Procedural law
    d.   Tort law

10. The making of new laws by a court is known as _____.
    a.   legislation
    b.   adjudication
    c.   judicial activism
    d.   judicial restraint

True/False Questions

T F 11. The first example of written law is the Code of Hammurabi.

T F 12. Rulings of the U.S. Supreme Court can be appealed to the President of the United States.

T F 13. *Mala* prohibitum offenses are illegal strictly because they have been defined as such by the law. They do not necessarily reflect widely-held social norms.

T F 14. The Law of the Twelve Tables is an example of influential law of the ancient Greek city-states.

T F 15. According to the text, one of the functions of law is dispute settlement.

Essay Questions

16. Discuss the basic assumptions of the natural law, consensus, and conflict models of law.

17. Where is law made? How is law made in each of the three branches of government (legislative, judicial, and executive)?

18. Why is the U.S. Supreme Court a uniquely influential court?

19.   Trace the development of law in America, through the colonial era to the present day. In what ways has American law been influenced by the English legal tradition?

20.   Discuss the necessary elements of a crime, and some typical defenses that are presented by criminal defendants in support of a plea of not guilty.

Answers to Sample Test Questions:

1d, 2a, 3b, 4c, 5a, 6b, 7b, 8c, 9b, 10c, 11T, 12F, 13T, 14F, 15T

CHAPTER FOUR
POLICING: HISTORY AND STRUCTURE

Learning Objectives

After completing this chapter, you should understand the following topics:

1. How methods of crime control in old England came to influence policing in colonial America.

2. How the London Metropolitan Police influenced the creation of permanent, paid police forces in the United States.

3. Changes in urban policing during the political era, the professional era, and the community policing era.

4. The structure of public policing in the United States, at local, state, and federal levels.

5. The increasing role played by private security and citizens.

6. Ways that policing is becoming increasingly international in scope.

Chapter Summary

1. Two major theoretical perspectives offer guidelines for our thinking about police. Consensus theory assumes that the police act on behalf of all citizens and groups to keep order and uphold the law. Conflict theory reminds us that the police can also protect the interests of powerful groups at the expense of poor and minority groups.

2. American policing has been influenced by methods developed in old England, which were brought to the American colonies by English settlers. The London Metropolitan Police, founded in 1829, was the model for subsequent development of full-time paid police agencies in the United States.

3. Policing in America has passed through three eras: the political era, the professional era, and the community policing era.

4. Public police are charged with primary responsibility for law enforcement and order maintenance. Their efforts are supplemented by individuals, community groups, and private security agencies.

5.   There are thousands of public police agencies in the United States, with jurisdiction at the local, state, and federal levels of government. The largest police departments are found in the nation's urban areas, but most rural and urban police departments have less than ten members.

6.   The private security industry has enjoyed rapid growth in the past two decades, with the number of private police now surpassing the number of public police.

7.   Policing is becoming increasingly international in scope, in order to respond to crimes that affect more than one nation.

Chapter Outline

The **Running Story in the Part 2 Opener** continues the case of Dawn Hamilton, a young girl who was murdered. In this installment of the story, students learn that a man named Kirk Bloodsworth has been arrested for the crime. Further installments in the running story appear in the openers to Parts 3, and 4 of the book. The running story illustrates the stages of the criminal justice process, and some of the issues and ambiguities surrounding criminal justice in America.

Introduction

A.   This chapter deals with **two fundamental questions**:

     1.   How did the idea of policing arise in Western history?

     2.   What forms does American policing take today?

B.   For most of human history, there were no **permanent, paid police** forces. This type of policing has only arisen in the past two hundred years.

C.   **Consensus theory** predicts that organized police will be unnecessary in primitive societies, where there is strong agreement on values and norms.

D.   **Conflict theory** predicts that police will be allied with powerful persons and groups.

I. Historical Influences

A.   Although there were some organized police in **ancient civilizations**, criminal prosecution has historically been carried out by the victim or the victim's family.

B.   In 1667, Nicholas-Gabriel de La Reynie was appointed Lieutenant of Police in Paris, **France**.

C.   In **England** after the time of Saxon King Alfred the Great (870-901), the people were responsible for keeping the King's peace under the **frankpledge system**.

   1.   Citizens raised the **hue and cry** and groups would then search for criminal suspects.

   2.   A **tithing** was made up of ten families. Ten tithings formed a **hundred**. After the Assize of 1181, all tithing members were required to be armed.

   3.   The **constable** played an early law enforcement role in the hundreds.

   4.   **Shire-reeves** emerged in the 10th century. Forerunner of the modern sheriff.

   5.   1285 - King Edward I created the **watch and ward** system to enforce law in the towns.

   6.   The office of **justice of the peace** was established in the early 1300s.

C.   During the American **colonial era** (1607-1776), law enforcement was carried out by constables, sheriffs, and the night watch.

II.   *The Rise of Modern Policing*

A.   **London** -

   1.   In 1693, Parliament agreed to pay citizens to act as **thief-takers.**

   2.   In 1753, Henry Fielding established the **Bow Street Runners**.

   3.   **The London Metropolitan Police** was the first modern police department in the English-speaking world (established 1829). Basic organizing principles:

      a.   government control of the police

      b.   basic mission of order maintenance and crime prevention

      c.   public approval as measure of police success

        d.   quasi-military structure

        e.   qualified and trained officers

        f.   probationary period for new recruits

        g.   management of resources by time and area

        h.   use of only minimum levels of force

B.   **First American Police Departments**, established on the London model:

    1.   **Boston** (1838)

    2.   **New York City** (1845)

    3.   Police departments created in the 19th century shared **four innovative characteristics**:

        a.   **hierarchical** organization

        b.   location within the **executive branch** of city government

        c.   adoption of a standard police **uniform**

        d.   **paid** officers.

C.   **Policing the American City**

    1.   During the **Political Policing Era** (1830-1900), ties between police and local political parties were strong.

    2.   Many **reforms** were initiated during the **Professional Policing Era** (1900-1965). Important roles were played by the **Wickersham Commission** (1929) and the **Federal Bureau of Investigation (FBI)** under J. Edgar Hoover.

        a.   reduction of political influence

        b.   appointment of qualified chiefs

        c.   higher personnel standards

        d.   scientific management principles

        e.   military-style discipline

        f.   creation of specialized police units

3.   The **Community Policing Era** (1965-Present) grew out of the civil unrest of the 1960s.

        a.   Herman Goldstein advocated **problem-oriented policing**, which focuses on broad community problems rather than specific criminal incidents.

        b.   James Q. Wilson and George Kelling: **broken windows hypothesis**. Signs of neglect serve notice that a neighborhood is in decline.

        c.   **Implications of community policing:** increased ties to community residents and groups, focus on neighborhood disorder of all types, increased use of foot patrol, police work is more closely with other agencies.

III.   *The Structure of American Policing*

There are thousands of police agencies in the United States, at the municipal, county, state, and federal levels. Policing is also carried out by private police and by citizens. Policing is becoming increasingly international in scope.

A.   Public Policing

1.   **Municipal (Local) Police** - Most police are municipal (local) police. They handle most of the crime and disorder that occurs in the United States.

2.   **Sheriffs** - Provide varied law enforcement services at the county level. Sheriffs are unique among police because they are elected rather than appointed. They work closely with courts.

3.   **State Police and Highway Patrols** - Patrol rural areas and highways, and assist local police with manpower, laboratories, specialized equipment, and training.

4. **Special Police** - Have jurisdiction over parks, airports, subways, colleges, harbors, housing areas, and other places. They may be employed at the local, county, state, or federal levels.

5. **Federal Law Enforcement** - The U.S. has no national police force, although the FBI has come closest from time to time. There are over 63 federal agencies with police powers (see Table 4.1 on page 114 in the text).

B. **Private Security** - Closely tied to corporate organizations.

1. Private police **outnumber** public police by about three to one.

2. **WAECUP:** Waste, Accidents, Errors, Crime, and Unethical Practices (Bottom and Kostanoski).

3. **Concerns** about private policing include accountability, hiring of private police by government agencies (privatization), and widening the net of social control.

C. **Citizen Policing** - Citizens perform policing in a number of different ways:

1. **Occasional avocational policing** - serving law enforcement in indirect ways, such as by reporting a crime.

2. **Obligatory avocational policing** - When citizens are legally required to use force. For example, assisting an officer who requests help.

3. **Volunteer avocational policing** - Examples include neighborhood watch groups and auxiliary police.

4. **Entrepreneurial avocational policing** - Policing for a profit. Examples include bail enforcement agents and paid informers.

D. **International Policing** - Crime is becoming increasingly international in scope (drugs, terrorism, economic crime) and policing is expanding to meet this condition. INTERPOL was formed in 1923 to assist police agencies with international investigations.

Key Terms

Bow Street Runners
community policing era
constable

entrepreneurial avocational policing
frankpledge system
hundred
INTERPOL
justice of the peace
obligatory avocational policing
occasional avocational policing
political policing era
problem-oriented policing
professional policing era
shire-reeve
thief-takers
tithing
volunteer avocational policing
WAECUP
watch and ward

Questions for Study

1. Describe how crime control was accomplished in old England and colonial America.

2. What made the London Metropolitan Police different from the methods of crime control in existence prior to that time?

3. How did American policing change during the political era, the professional era, and the community policing era?

4. Describe the structure of public policing at local, state, and federal levels of government.

5. What functions do private security employees perform?

6. In what ways do citizens perform crime control tasks?

Selected Readings

William C. Cunningham, John J. Strauchs, and Clifford W. Van Meter, Private Security Trends 1970-2000: The Hallcrest Report II (Stoneham, MA: Butterworth-Heinemann, 1990). Profiles the scope of private security in America during the last quarter of the 20th century.

Robert M. Fogelson, Big-City Police (Cambridge, MA: Harvard University Press, 1977). A social history of American police reform in the 20th century.

Roger Lane, Policing the City: Boston 1822-1885 (Cambridge, MA: Harvard University Press, 1967). Along with Richardson's The New York Police, Lane's book is a classic of American police history.

Tony Poveda, Lawlessness and Reform: The FBI in Transition (Pacific Grove, California: Brooks/Cole, 1990). Poveda places the history of the FBI in social and historical context, with particular emphasis on changes taking place after J. Edgar Hoover's death in 1972.

James F. Richardson, The New York Police: Colonial Times to 1901, (New York: Oxford University Press, 1970). A classic discussion of the rise of the nation's largest police department.

Michael Tonry and Norval Morris (eds.), Modern Policing - Crime and Justice: A Review of Research (Chicago: University of Chicago Press, 1992). A volume from an influential annual series. Contains ten in-depth chapters by some of America's leading scholars of the police.

Samuel Walker, A Critical History of Police Reform (Lexington, MA: Lexington, 1977). An examination of the history of police in the United States from the formation of the first departments through 1940. Walker pays particular attention to processes of reform and the rise of professionalism.

Sample Test Questions

Multiple Choice Questions

1.   Under the frankpledge system in old England, a tithing was _____.
     a.   an organization of ten families
     b.   a tax on crops produced on rented land
     c.   a donation to the Church
     d.   an early type of law enforcement officer

2.   According to the consensus perspective, permanent and paid police agencies developed because _____.
     a.   old methods of law enforcement had become obsolete
     b.   the lower class was becoming an increasing threat
     c.   fearsome robbers were roaming the highways
     d.   (all of the above)

3. According to your text, the American colonial era began with _____.
    a. the arrival of the *Mayflower*
    b. the signing of the Declaration of Independence
    c. the drafting of the U.S. Constitution
    d. the settlement of Jamestown

4. The Bow Street Runners were formed in 1753 by London Magistrate

    _____.
    a. William Blackstone
    b. Henry Fielding
    c. Alexander Maconochie
    d. Robert Peel

5. In 1929, the Wickersham Commission exposed the existence of a police investigative practice known as _____.
    a. thumping
    b. the third degree
    c. four-packs
    d. the screen test

6. The _____ hypothesis suggests that visible signs of neighborhood neglect can increase crime by serving notice that the area is in decline.
    a. differential association
    b. XYY
    c. broken windows
    d. urban renewal

7. Which of the following models of private security discussed by Clifford Shearing suggests that policing can best be accomplished by public and private police?
    a. state-centered model
    b. laissez-faire model
    c. pluralist model
    d. · egalitarian model

8. *In small and primitive social groups, community solidarity is high and police are unnecessary.* This statement is most consistent with which of the following theoretical approaches?
    a. consensus
    b. conflict
    c. interactionist
    d. radical

9. In 1285, _____ decreed that English villages post a watch at the gates during night hours.
    a. the Decree of 1285
    b. the Statute of Kensington
    c. the Magna Carta
    d. the Statute of Winchester

10. Which of the following is a hallmark of the professional policing era in the United States?
    a. appointment of qualified personnel
    b. military-style discipline
    c. scientific management principles
    d. (all of the above)

True/False Questions

T F 11. The social turbulence and unrest of the late 1960s led to the adoption of the professional policing model in America.

T F 12. With the possible exception of the FBI, the United States has no national police force with general law enforcement powers throughout the country.

T F 13. If a police officer asks a motorist to assist at a traffic accident, then the motorist is engaging in occasional avocational policing.

T F 14. Herman Goldstein's idea of problem-oriented policing suggests that police should focus more of their attention and resources on the problem of serious crime.

T F 15. Most police officers in the United States are employed at the local or municipal level.

Essay Questions

16. Discuss the history of permanent, paid police in England and America. Why is such a police force needed, according to Carl Klockers?

17. What agencies make up the structure of policing in the United States, at municipal, county, state, and federal levels?

18. What role do private security and citizen policing play in the overall picture of policing in American society?

19. How has American policing changed as it passed through the political policing era, the professional policing era, and now the community policing era?

20. Discuss the community policing model, from the points of view of the consensus approach and the conflict approach.

Answers to Sample Test Questions

1a. 2a, 3d, 4b, 5b, 6c, 7c, 8a, 9d, 10d, 11F, 12T, 13F, 14F, 15T

CHAPTER FIVE
FUNCTIONS OF POLICING AND THE POLICE OFFICER ROLE

Learning Objectives

After completing this chapter, you should understand the following topics:

1. The functions and responsibilities of policing.

2. The nature of police tasks: operations, administration, and auxiliary services.

3. How the police role is influenced by discretion, the myth of crime prevention, and the community policing model.

4. The special situations of women and minority officers.

5. How officers learn the norms and values of the police role.

6. How the public learns about police.

Chapter Summary

1. According to the consensus approach, the functions of policing in a democratic society are law enforcement, order maintenance, and service. Conflict theory looks at which groups benefit, and which groups suffer, when the police work toward meeting these goals.

2. Routine police tasks are divided into three areas: operations, administration and auxiliary services. Operational areas include patrol, traffic, criminal investigation, juvenile affairs, vice/organized crime/intelligence, and community services/crime prevention. Administration and auxiliary services provide support for police operations.

3. Research has called into question a number of key assumptions about police operations, such as the effectiveness of motorized patrol, the need for rapid response, and the role of detectives in criminal investigation.

4. The keystone assumption of policing--that police activities can affect levels of crime--has itself been questioned. Many scholars now believe that the police can have little effect on crime rates since most causes of crime are beyond their control.

5. Police need to use a great deal of discretion on the job.

6.   The police role has been influenced by the community policing model, which broadens the scope of policing to include community disorder and other problems.

7.   Police organizations have traditionally been white and male. More women and minorities are becoming police, but they still experience difficulties.

8.   Policing is a career. Recruits learn about their job through the process of socialization. Ideas about police in the wider society are strongly influenced by the popular media. Police continue their socialization at the training academy and on the job.

Chapter Outline

Introduction

This chapter focuses on **three questions**:

1.   What **should** the police do?

2.   What activities do they **actually perform**?

3.   How are police officers **selected and trained**?

Consensus theory suggests that the police maintain order for the benefit of all. **Conflict theory** suggests that police activities may favor powerful groups.

I.   *What Police Should Do.* Why do police seem necessary?

The single most important aspect of the police role is the **right to use force**.

A.   **Functions** of policing (beneficial consequences for social order):

    1.   **Manifest functions** (intended outcomes)

        a.   law enforcement

        b.   order maintenance

        c.   service to the community

    2.   Important **latent functions** (unintended consequences) include providing jobs for police and economic benefits for communities.

B. Egon Bittner suggests that police are needed in situations where *"something-ought-not-to-be-happening-and-about-which-someone-had-better-do-something-now!"*

C. **Specific Responsibilities** of police (American Bar Association)

1. Prevent and control conduct widely recognized as threatening to life and property (**serious crime**)

2. **Aid individuals** who are in danger of physical harm

3. **Protect constitutional guarantees**, such as the rights of free speech and assembly

4. Facilitate the **movement** of people and vehicles

5. Assist those who **cannot care for themselves**

6. Resolve **conflict**

7. Identify **problems** that have the potential for becoming more serious dilemmas for the individual citizen, for the police, or for the government

8. Create and maintain a **feeling of security** in the community

9. Promote and preserve **civil order**

10. Provide **other services** on an emergency basis.

II. *What Police Do: Activities and Workload*

At the level of the police organization, there are **three primary tasks**:

1. **Operations**

2. **Administration**

3. **Auxiliary services**

A. **Assumptions and Realities**

1. **Research** has examined long-held assumptions that police can control crime, and that they spend most of their time in crime control efforts.

2. Studies suggest that police spend **most of their time on order maintenance** activities rather than on direct crime control.

3. For individual officers, police work consists of the **assignments** they are given, the **situations** they encounter, and the **outcomes** that they initiate in order to discharge their duties.

B. **Police Operations: Patrol**

Most police officers are assigned to patrol duty.

1. **Research on Patrol Effectiveness**.

    a. The **Kansas City Preventive Patrol Study** (1972) suggested that changing levels of police patrol does not affect the amount of crime or citizens' fear of crime.

    b. **The Kansas City Response Time Study** (1978) concluded that fast police response has little or no relationship to the likelihood of arresting a suspect.

    c. Studies suggest that the major factor in whether an arrest is made is the **amount of time citizens wait** before calling the police.

    d. These studies showed that **common sense assumptions can be wrong**. They must be tested by research.

2. **Foot Patrol and the Fear of Crime**

    a. The **Newark Foot Patrol Experiment** (1981) found that foot patrol does not seem to affect crime rates, but it makes citizens **feel safer**.

    b. Research by Trojanowicz suggests that foot patrol makes **police officers feel safer**, as well.

C. **Other Operations**

1. **Criminal Investigation** - identifying suspects and gathering evidence against them that can be presented in court.

    a.   Detectives' investigations consist of **5 steps**:

        1.   **establish** the case

        2.   **identify** a suspect

        3.   **locate** the suspect

        4.   **interview** the suspect

        5.   **disposing** of the case

    b.   Research has called into question **3 traditional assumptions** about investigation of crimes:

        1.   that the majority of **crimes can be solved** by the police

        2.   that detective work consists primarily of locating **criminals who are unknown** at the start of an investigation

        3.   that **each criminal case should be investigated** to the fullest extent.

2.   **Traffic Regulation -**

    a.   keeping people and vehicles **moving**

    b.   enforcing laws dealing with **traffic, vehicles, and parking**

    c.   enforcing **speed limits**

    d.   enforcing **driving-while-intoxicated** laws

    e.   responding to **traffic accidents**

3.   **Vice Crime/Organized Crime/Intelligence -**

    a.   **vice crimes** are often called "victimless crimes"

        1.   gambling

        2.   prostitution

3.   illegal pornography

4.   illegal liquor and tobacco sales

b.   **Organized crime** enterprises are often engaged in vice crimes. Policing is hampered because there is a large public demand for access to vice activities.

c.   Police **intelligence** activities involve gathering evidence, often using **undercover** techniques.

4.   **Juvenile Affairs** - Young persons are processed differently than adults, because the law assumes that they are incapable of full criminal responsibility.

a.   **Delinquency** is crimes committed by juveniles.

b.   **Status offenses** are activities that are prohibited for juveniles but not for adults, such as drinking, certain sexual activity, running away from home, truancy, and others.

5.   **Community Service and Crime Prevention** - The police are available 24 hours a day, 7 days a week. They perform a variety of services, and work to prevent crime whenever possible.

D.   **Support Tasks**

1.   **Administration** involves day-to-day management of the police organization (personnel, budgeting, financial affairs, research, legal work, public relations, office paperwork, and so on).

2.   **Auxiliary services** include specialized tasks that aid police operations and administration (records management, communication, property control, laboratory services, lockup of suspects, fingerprinting, drug and alcohol testing, and so on).

III.   *How Police Work*

A.   Nearly every situation encountered by police officers requires them to use **discretion** (judgment). A **core decision** is whether or not to invoke the law (make an arrest).

1.   The **myth of full enforcement** is the mistaken belief that police enforce all laws equally.

2.   James Q. Wilson uncovered various **police department styles** in a study of six American cities:

   a.   **Watchman style** - order maintenance is considered to be the primary police responsibility.

   b.   **Legalistic style** - emphasis is placed on uniform enforcement of all laws.

   c.   **Service style** - emphasis on maintaining good relations with the community.

B.   **The Myth of Crime Prevention** - Very little police time and resources are focused on crime prevention. Instead, police tend to focus on crime and disorder that has **already occurred**. Crime prevention is a task for society as a whole. However, American culture sees the police as **responsible** for crime.

C.   **The Community Policing Model** - A new approach that grew out of dissatisfaction with police handling of the urban disorder in the 1960s. (See table 5.3 on page 144 for comparison of traditional and community policing).

1.   There is **no single accepted definition** of community policing.

2.   In general, community policing involves **closer ties** to community groups, and a shift from focus on criminal incidents to a **focus on broad problems** of community disorder.

3.   James Q. Wilson and George Kelling's **Broken Windows** hypothesis - small signs of neighborhood disorder send the message that residents no longer care. Crime rates then rise.

4.   Herman Goldstein's **Problem-Oriented Policing** advocates that police should focus on broad community problems rather than on discrete incidents.

5.   The **effectiveness** of community policing is currently unknown, and further research is required.

IV. *Who Police Officers Are*

There are about 750,000 police officers in the United States. Another 1.5 million are employed in private security. Officers have traditionally been members of the working class, with a high school education or less. Most have been males. All of this is now changing.

A. **Should Police Have a College Education?** As of 1988, over 75 percent of police officers had attended college. There is widespread support among police chiefs for higher educational standards for officers.

B. **Women in a Traditionally Male Occupation**.

    1. First fully empowered police officer in the nation was **Alice Stebbins Wells**, appointed to the Los Angeles Police Department in 1910.

    2. Women make up only about **9 percent** of the nation's police officers.

    3. Studies show women officers to be **equally as effective** as males.

    4. Woman officers still face **resistance from male colleagues**, although this situation may be changing for the better.

C. **Minority Police Officers** are still under represented relative to their percentage in the population as a whole.

    1. Many police agencies now actively **strive to hire minority officers**.

    2. The **Civil Rights Act of 1964** allowed police departments to be sued on the grounds of discrimination in employment practices.

V. *Policing as an Occupation*

A. **Socialization** - Internalizing the **values and norms** of policing, and developing a sense of police **identity**.

    1. Socialization of police occurs in 3 arenas:

        a. in the **popular culture**

        b. in the **training academy**

        c. **on the job**

B. **Career Stages** - According to Samuel Walker, the stages of an officer's career include:

1. application

2. screening

3. selection

4. academy training

5. probationary period

6. promotion

7. retirement, resignation, or termination

C. **Learning From Experience** - According to David Bayley, experience teaches police officers about operating goals, tactics, and presence.

1. **Operating Goals:**

   a. how to conform to the **norms** of the department

   b. how to manage physically **dangerous** persons and situations

   c. how to **prevent** criminal activity

   d. how to minimize the **dangers** of the job

   e. how to **avoid antagonizing** members of the public

2. **Tactics:**

   a. how to manage **initial contact** with citizens

   b. how to **proceed** with required actions

   c. how to **exit** from incidents

3. **Presence:** external calm and internal alertness, to keep control of the situation and minimize danger.

D.   **The Media** represents a powerful influence on our ideas of policing. Much media portrayal of police activity is inaccurate.

E.   **The Police Subculture -**

      1.   First identified by **William Westley** in 1950. Mistrust of the public, secretiveness, cynicism, protection of fellow officers.

      2.   Police **working personality** - assumptions and ways of thinking that officers adopt while on the job. Influenced by the elements of **danger** and **authority**.

Key Terms

assignments, situations, and outcomes
community policing
community service function
crime control function
discretion
operating goals, tactics, and presence
order maintenance function
police operations
police subculture
police socialization
police working personality
problem-oriented policing

Questions for Study

1.   What should the police do? What do they actually do?

2.   Relatively how much police office time is spent on crime fighting, order maintenance, and service?

3.   What do scholars mean when they say that police can probably have little effect on levels of crime?

4.   What activities are covered by the term "police operations?"

5.   What is police discretion, and what factors influence they ways that it is exercised?

6.   What special circumstances have affected women and minority officers?

7.   What typical stages does an officer pass through during his or her career?

Selected Readings

David H. Bayley, <u>Police for the Future</u>, (New York: Oxford University Press, 1994). Bayley examines policing in Australia, Great Britain, Canada, Japan, and the United States. He presents a theory of policing in democratic society.

Connie Fletcher, <u>What Cops Know: Cops Talk About What They Do, How They Do It, and What It Does to Them</u>, (New York: Villard, 1991). A highly readable and informative book based on journalist Fletcher's interviews with Chicago police officers.

Herman Goldstein, <u>Policing a Free Society</u>, (Cambridge, MA: Ballinger, 1977). A classic discussion of the social context of policing.

Carl B. Klockars, <u>The Idea of Police</u>, (Newbury Park, CA: Sage, 1985). A short essay in which the author justifies society's need for full time, paid police.

Peter K. Manning, <u>Police Work: The Social Organization of Policing</u>, (Cambridge, MA: MIT Press, 1977). One of the most sociologically sophisticated treatments of policing and the police.

Dennis P. Rosenbaum, ed., <u>The Challenge of Community Policing: Testing the Promises</u>, (Thousand Oaks, CA: Sage, 1994). A comprehensive collection of articles on the theory and practice of community policing in the United States and abroad.

Sample Test Questions

Multiple Choice Questions

1.   Which of the following is NOT a manifest function of policing?
    a.   law enforcement
    b.   order maintenance
    c.   service
    d.   (all of the above are manifest functions of policing)

2.   Which of the following assumptions has been called into question by criminal justice research?
    a.   motorized automobile patrol reduces crime
    b.   rapid response to calls increases arrest rates
    c.   detectives solve most crimes with information they gather themselves
    d.   (all of the above assumptions have been called into question)

3. For individual police officers, police work consists of assignments, situations, and
   _____.
   a. tasks
   b. patrol
   c. investigations
   d. outcomes

4. _____ is the individual judgement that police officers use in choosing from a broad array of alternatives to employ in situations encountered on the job.
   a. detention
   b. training
   c. discretion
   d. interdiction

5. About what percentage of the nation's municipal police officers are women?
   a. 9 percent
   b. 19 percent
   c. 39 percent
   d. 59 percent

6. _____ is a group of occupational assumptions and ways of thinking that police officers adopt on the job.
   a. The police outlook
   b. The police working attitude
   c. The police working personality
   d. The police officer's creed

7. Research shows that women police officers are _____ male officers.
   a. less effective than
   b. as effective as
   c. more effective than
   d. (research has not addressed this question)

8. According to sociologist William Westley, police officer groups tend to be mistrustful, secretive, cynical, and protective of fellow officers. Westley calls this constellation of group norms _____.
   a. the police subculture
   b. the self fulfilling prophecy
   c. the police secret society
   d. the officer's working norms

9.   Where do police officers learn how to perform the occupational role of policing?
   a.   from the popular culture
   b.   in the training academy
   c.   on the job
   d.   (all of the above)

10.   Most police officers are assigned to _____.
   a.   investigation
   b.   juvenile affairs
   c.   foot patrol
   d.   motorized patrol

True/False Questions

T F 11.   Police officers participate in an average of 7 shootings per year, nationwide.

T F 12.   The manifest functions of policing are law enforcement, order maintenance, and service.

T F 13.   Patrol, traffic, criminal investigation, juvenile affairs, vice/organized crime/intelligence, and community service/crime prevention all fall into the category of police tasks known as auxiliary services.

T F 14.   The Kansas City Preventive Patrol Experiment showed that increased levels of motorized automobile patrol are associated with measurable decreases in the level of violent crime and property crime.

T F 15.   According to the text, the factor that most distinguishes policing from other occupations is the uniform that police officers wear.

Essay Questions

16.   Discuss the situation of women and minority group members in policing. How is the situation for these officers different now than it was in the past? Do women and minority officers still experience difficulties on the job that are related to their minority group status?

17.   The consensus approach enumerates several manifest and latent functions of policing. What are some of the functions of policing?

18.   Police organizations are organized around the tasks of operations, administration, and auxiliary services. Explain how police organizations are structured in order to accomplish these tasks.

19. Research studies have called into question a number of long-held assumptions about policing. Discuss these studies, and their implications for allocation of police resources.

20. Compare and contrast the community policing model with the traditional way of thinking about police. In what ways is community policing like the older methods? In what ways is it different?

Answers to Sample Test Questions

1d, 2d, 3d, 4c, 5a, 6c, 7b, 8a, 9d, 10d, 11F, 12T, 13F, 14F, 15F

CHAPTER SIX
CRITICAL ISSUES IN POLICING

Learning Objectives

After completing this chapter, you should understand the following topics:

1. How the consensus and conflict perspectives provide insight into police procedures and police misconduct.

2. Constitutional limits on police behavior relating to search and seizure, detention, identification, and interrogation of criminal suspects.

3. Types of police corruption and abuse of authority

4. Theories about why police misconduct exists.

5. How police misconduct affects relations between police and members of minority groups.

6. Ways of increasing police accountability.

7. Dangers and difficulties facing the police, including stress, illness, and the threat of violence.

Chapter Summary

1. The consensus and conflict perspectives help us understand the issues discussed in this chapter. The consensus view assumes that police officers share the values of the wider society, and that police activities benefit all groups equally. The conflict approach sees police as a powerful interest group that may attempt to dominate members of less powerful groups.

2. Police must also be particularly careful to protect suspects' Constitutional rights in the areas of search and seizure, detention, identification, and interrogation.

3. Evidence that has been improperly obtained is inadmissible in court, under the exclusionary rule.

4. Police misconduct consists of corruption and abuse of authority. Theories of police misconduct emphasize the role played by social factors.

5. Although police are granted the right to use force, they are sometimes accused of using excessive force or unjustified deadly force.

6.   Police misconduct strains relations with minority groups.

7.   Strategies for accountability include political change, civil suits, citizen review boards and police department internal methods.

8.   Dangers faced by the police include stress, illness, and violence. FBI data show that dozens of police officers are killed in the line of duty each year.

Chapter Outline

Introduction

The topics examined in this chapter--**rights of suspects** and **police misconduct**--clearly illustrate the divergent approaches of consensus theory and conflict theory.

A.   **Consensus**: How do police procedures help to control crime for the benefit of all members of society?

B.   **Conflict:** What does the existence of police corruption and brutality tell us about relations between the haves and the have nots in American society?

I.   *Police Procedure and the Rights of Suspects*

The **power of the police is not unlimited**. Police officers are responsible for protecting suspects' constitutional rights.

The **U.S. Constitution** enumerates the rights of criminal suspects primarily in the 4th, 5th, 6th, 8th, and 14th amendments.

A.   **Search and Seizure** (4th Amendment)

1.   **Warrants**

2.   **Probable cause**

3.   **"Fruit of the poisoned tree" doctrine**

4.   **Exclusionary rule**

a.   *Weeks v. United States* (1914)

b.   *Mapp v. Ohio* (1961)

5.   **Exceptions** to the Exclusionary rule:

    a.   Good faith exception

    b.   inevitable discovery exception

    c.   purged taint exception

    d.   independent source exception

6.   A **warrant is not required** in certain situations:

    a.   searches incident to arrest

    b.   searches conducted with the consent of the suspect

    d.   searches conducted on an emergency basis

    d.   cursory stop-and-frisk searches

    e.   inventory searches of automobiles after arrest

    f.   items in plain view

    g.   searches in prisons and jails

    h.   searches by nongovernmental agents

B.   **Detention** - three levels

1.   **Stop and frisk**

    a.   *Terry v. Ohio* (1968)

2.   **Station house detention**

3.   **Arrest**

C.   **Identification** (5th Amendment)

1.   **Lineup**

2.   **Showup**

        3.   **Polygraph examination** (lie detector test)

        4.   **Hypnosis**

   D.   **Interrogation** (5th Amendment)

        1.   *Miranda v. Arizona*

II.   *Police Misconduct*

Most police officers **do not engage in police misconduct**, although many temptations are built into the nature of the job.

Most U.S. residents rate the **ethical standards of police quite high**--about the same as college teachers.

   A.   **Corruption** - Illegal activity for monetary gain. Possible types (Roebuck and Barker):

        1.   **Corruption of authority**

        2.   **Kickbacks**

        3.   **Opportunistic theft**

        4.   **Shakedowns**

        5.   **Protection of Illegal activities**

        6.   **The "fix"**

        7.   **Direct criminal activities**

        8.   **Internal payoffs**

Another type of corruption is **lying**. Not all lying is seen as unacceptable (Barker and Carter)

        1.   **Accepted lying** - ex. adopting a false identity in an undercover investigation

        2.   **Tolerated lying** - seen as undesirable but necessary

3. **Deviant lying** - violating police procedure and sometimes the law. Ex. lying on the stand in court ("testi-lying").

B. **Abuse of Authority** - Verbal or physical acts by the police that unjustly injure, threaten, demean, or violate the rights of persons.

    1. **Excessive Force (brutality)** - ex. Rodney King (1991). Most police contacts with citizens involve little or no violence.

    2. **Police-Minority Relations** - Police relations with minority groups are often tense

        a. Police relations with Black Americans have historically been poor

        b. Rap music provides a statement of some minority youth's view of the police in the inner city.

    3. **Deadly Force** - Police are granted the right to use deadly force when necessary. Most police killings of suspects are justified, but some are not.

        a. Common Law Fleeing Felon Rule - no longer in effect

        b. *Tennessee v. Garner* (1985) - Limited officer's right to shoot at suspects

C. **Theories of Police Misconduct** - Three hypotheses:

    1. **Society-at-Large hypothesis** - Influence of strong social norms. ex. value of economic success.

    2. **Structural or Affiliation hypothesis** - Influence of police subcultural values and norms.

    3. **Rotten-Apple hypothesis** - A small number of "rotten" officers corrupt the whole "barrel" of other officers in a department.

These hypotheses adopt an implicit **consensus view**, because they assume that there is a single standard of right and wrong. The **conflict approach** sees officers as an interest group that may be opposed to others (suspects, minorities, and others).

    D.   **Accountability** - Examining the actions of police. Walker sees four ways this might be accomplished:

        1.   **Political change** - ex. creation of civil service laws

        2.   **The courts** - Rulings of appeals courts, civil litigation against officers

        3.   **Civilian review** - A board made up of citizens from the community

        4.   **Internal methods** - ex. better training, tangible rewards, internal affairs units

III.   *Dangers and Difficulties* - Policing can be a stressful and dangerous occupation.

    A.   **Stress and Illness**

        1.   Concept of **stress** proposed by Dr. Hans Selye in 1956. Stress not always negative.

        2.   Stress affects some officers **more than others**.

    B.   **Risk of Violence -**

        1.   Statistically, one American police **officer is killed** every three days.

        2.   The **most dangerous type of call** is investigating suspicious persons or circumstances, and ambush.

Key Terms

abuse of authority
citizen review boards
corruption
detention
due process
exclusionary rule
fleeing felon doctrine
identification
interrogation
kickback
opportunistic theft
police accountability
probable cause

rotten apple hypothesis
search and seizure
shakedown
society-at-large hypothesis
stop and frisk
structural (affiliation) hypothesis
warrant

Questions for Study

1.   Why are the 4th, 5th, 6th, 8th and 14th Amendments to the U.S. Constitution particularly important for criminal justice? (See Appendix C for the complete text of these amendments).

2.   Why is the concept of probable cause important for police work?

3.   What is the exclusionary rule? What are some exceptions to it?

4.   Discuss the various types of police corruption and abuse of authority. What are some theoretical explanations of why police misconduct occurs?

5.   What strategies have been proposed to hold the police accountable to the public?

6.   Discuss some of the dangers that police officers face, including stress, illness, and violence.

Selected Readings and Resources

Paul Chevigny, Police Violence in the Americas (New York: New Press, 1995). An examination of police violence in the United States, Latin America, and the Caribbean.

Rolando V. del Carmen, Criminal Procedure: Law and Practice, 4th ed. (Belmont, CA: Wadsworth, 1998). An authoritative examination of legal issues and court cases bearing on criminal justice procedure.

National Institute of Justice, Crime File Videotape Series (Washington, D.C.: U.S. Department of Justice). A series of 38 half-hour videotapes, covering some of the most pressing issues in criminal justice today. Most tapes are directly or indirectly related to policing.

PBS Video, Eyes on the Prize and Eyes on the Prize II, (Alexandria, VA: PBS Video, 1986 and 1990). A stunning series of one-hour videotapes that traces the American civil rights movement from the 1950s to the present. Several episodes focus on police/minority relations.

Douglas W. Perez, <u>Common Sense About Police Review</u> (Philadelphia: Temple University Press, 1994). A study of police review systems in five locations across the United States. Perez concludes that, to be effective, police review must involve approaches that are both external and internal to police organizations.

Jerome H. Skolnick and James J. Fyfe, <u>Above the Law: Police and the Excessive Use of Force</u> (New York: Free Press, 1993). An examination of police brutality in America.

Malcolm K. Sparrow, Mark H. Moore, and David M. Kennedy, <u>Beyond 911: A New Era for Policing</u> (Basic Books, 1990). Presents the argument that police can be effective in combating crime and reducing fear by thinking of their task in new ways.

Sample Test Questions

Multiple Choice Questions

1. _____ is unorganized and unplanned theft by police during the course of their routine duties.
    a. The fix
    b. Internal payoffs
    c. Opportunistic theft
    d. Protection of illegal activities

2. Verbal or physical acts by the police that unjustly injure, threaten, demean, or violate the rights of persons is _____.
    a. tolerated lying
    b. the fix
    c. corruption
    d. abuse of authority

3. In which of the following cases did the Supreme Court rule that the exclusionary rule applies in state court as well as in federal court?
    a. *Terry v. Ohio*
    b. *Weeks v. United States*
    c. *Mapp v. Ohio*
    d. *Miranda v. Arizona*

4. Which of the following hypotheses suggests that a small number of corrupt officers will influence other police officers to participate in illegal activity?
    a. society-at-large
    b. structural or affiliation
    c. rotten-apple
    d. training

5.   A _____ is a legal document, approved by a judge, that gives police officers permission for a search or arrest.
  a.   citation
  b.   warrant
  c.   summons
  d.   ticket

6.   A panel of community members who are charged with overseeing the police and reviewing allegations of misconduct is a(n) _____.
  a.   internal affairs board
  b.   citizen review board
  c.   Congressional oversight committee
  d.   neighborhood citizens' council

7.   According to the Gallup Poll, black Americans tend to feel that the criminal justice process treats blacks _____ than whites.
  a.   more harshly
  b.   about the same
  c.   more leniently

8.   Lying by police officers is _____.
  a.   acceptable
  b.   wrong
  c.   tolerated
  d.   (it depends on the situation)

9.   Which of the following is a responsibility of police officers?
  a.   gathering evidence to use in court against suspects
  b.   protecting the rights of criminal suspects
  c.   testifying in court
  d.   (all of the above)

10.   Research indicates that most police contacts with citizens involve _____ violence.
  a.   little or no
  b.   some
  c.   a great deal of
  d.   (research has not addressed this issue)

True/False Questions

T F 11.   FBI data indicate that dozens of police officers are killed in the line of duty each year.

T F 12.   The 4th Amendment to the Constitution contains the right to be free from unreasonable search and seizure.

T F 13.   Stop-and-frisk, station house detention, and arrest are essentially the same thing. That is, each involves about the same level of detention.

T F 14.   Stress is nearly always a bad thing for the human body.

T F 15.   Members of the public rate the ethical standards of police officers quite highly-- about the same as college teachers.

Essay Questions

16.   Policing can be a difficult and dangerous occupation. Discuss some myths and realities associated with policing as an occupation.

17.   Name three theoretical hypotheses that have been proposed to explain police misconduct, and discuss the basic assumptions of each.

18.   What actions constitute abuse of police authority, according to the text? How does abuse of authority affect the relations between the police and minority groups?

19.   Discuss the concept of probable cause, and its relation to police searches and seizures. How is search and seizure affected by the exclusionary rule?

20.   In what ways does the Constitution place limits on the behavior of police in the areas of search and seizure, detention, identification, and interrogation? Which constitutional amendments articulate the rights of criminal suspects in these areas?

Answers to Sample Test Questions:

1c, 2d, 3c, 4c, 5b, 6b, 7a, 8d, 9d, 10a, 11T, 12T, 13F, 14F, 15T

CHAPTER SEVEN
CRIMINAL COURTS: HISTORY AND STRUCTURE

Learning Objectives

After completing this chapter, you should understand the following topics:

1. Consensus and conflict perspectives on criminal courts: the functions that criminal courts serve (consensus), and ways that courts protect the interests of powerful groups (conflict).

2. How American colonial courts were influenced by English judicial practices and by factors unique to the American experience.

3. The structure of federal and state courts in the American dual court system.

4. The importance of other types of courts, including military courts-martial, Native American courts, and international tribunals.

5. The structure and process of court administration in the United States.

6. Strategies that have been used to reform state and federal courts in recent years.

Chapter Summary

1. Courts provide a forum where disputes may be resolved without bloodshed. Criminal courts determine the guilt (or lack of guilt) of criminal suspects, and they assign punishment upon conviction.

2. Consensus theory leads us to examine the functions that courts perform, while conflict theory shows us how courts can be influenced by matters of power and politics.

3. Courts are the oldest criminal justice agency--appearing in history long before prisons and permanent police forces. Historically, American courts were influenced by judicial practices brought from old England by the colonists. These practices were adapted to unique situations found in the New World.

4. The United States has a dual court structure, consisting of state and federal courts. In actuality there are 51 unique court structures, which makes it difficult to generalize about them.

5.   There are three levels of courts in the federal and state systems: courts of limited jurisdiction, courts of general jurisdiction, and appellate courts. Each state and the federal government has a court of last resort, which is its highest appeals court.

6.   Criminal matters are also adjudicated in special courts such as military courts-martial, Native American courts, and international tribunals. There is currently no permanent international criminal court.

7.   Court administration is carried out by chief judges, court administrators, and court clerks.

8.   Efforts to reform the courts have focused on court unification, centralization, and speedy trial legislation.

Chapter Outline

The **Running Story in the Part 3 Opener** continues the case of Dawn Hamilton, a young girl who was murdered. In this installment of the story, we learn that suspect Kirk Bloodsworth has been convicted after trial, and sentenced to death. After an appeal and a second trial, Bloodsworth is convicted again and sentenced to two life terms. The final installment in the running story appears in the opener to Part 4 of the book. The running story illustrates the stages of the criminal justice process, and some of the issues and ambiguities surrounding criminal justice in America.

Introduction

A.   Courts provide a **substitute for private vengeance**.

B.   The government **reserves criminal justice to itself**. Crimes are offenses against the state.

I.   *The Idea of Courts*

Criminal courts determine guilt and appropriate punishments (sentences). **Civil courts** assign liability and award monetary damages.

Adjudication: The process whereby a formal judicial decision is made and a sentence handed down.

Courts differ along 5 dimensions:

1.   **Legal culture** - the place the courts occupy in society

        a.   Mass legal culture - how the majority of society views courts

        b.   Elite legal culture - persons at the top of courts and the law

   2.   **Structure** - number of courts, jurisdictions (federal, state, local), and levels (lower, trial, appellate)

   3.   **Personnel** - persons who do the work of courts (judges, defense attorneys, prosecutors, and others)

   4.   **Scope of authority** - how many people do the court's decisions influence?

   5.   **Links with other political institutions** - links with executive and legislative branches

A.   **Consensus Theory**: The **functions** of Courts (good things that courts do for society as a whole)

   1.   **Settling disputes** - without bloodshed

   2.   Acting as **agencies of criminal justice** - determine guilt and assign punishment

   3.   Upholding the **legitimacy of government** - symbols of the moral correctness of law. Sites of ritual punishment.

   4.   Acting as **agents of social change** - examples are abortion rights, school desegregation, prison reform

B.   **Conflict Theory: Protecting the Powerful**

   1.   Law is seen as an expression of the **capitalist economic structure**. Law is a tool of the ruling class (Quinney). Courts tend to apply law in favor of the haves and against the interests of the have nots.

   2.   Example - Many of the 1989 **Tianenmen Square** demonstrators (People's Republic of China) were forced to undergo **show trials**, which reaffirmed authority of China's rulers over the people.

II.   *Historical Influences*

Courts are the **oldest criminal justice structures**, existing before police and prisons/jails.

A.   Courts in **Ancient Civilizations** -

     1.   **Ancient Israel** - "Court at the Gate" with clan elders. During the reign of King David (1010-970 B.C.), court was held in the temple at Jerusalem.

     2.   **Ancient Greece** - In Athens (5th century B. C.)

         a.   Serious criminal charges heard by **court of magistrates**

         b.   Lesser criminal charges processed in **dicastery courts**, with juries of up to 50 citizens

     3.   **Roman Empire** - (c. 500 B.C. - 500 A.D.)

         a.   Two types of magistrates (judges) heard criminal cases: **praetors** and **quaestors**. Members of the noble class.

         b.   **Plebeians** (common people) created **council of tribunes** (*concilium plebis*).

         c.   In later years, these were replaced by repressive **police courts**, which responded to threats against the emperor.

B.   The Emergence of **Courts in Old England**

     1.   Courts existed at time of victory by **William the Conqueror** over the Anglo-Saxons in 1066 (Battle of Hastings).

         a.   **Hundred court** - concentrated on civil disputes

         b.   **Shire court** - heard criminal cases

         c.   **King's justices** - traveled to shires to hold court

         d.   **Seignorial court** (manorial court) - resolved disputes on feudal manors

         e.   **Magna Curia** (Kings Council) - heard serious criminal cases

         f.   **Justices of the Peace** - early 14th century. Heard minor criminal matters. More serious cases held for visit of the **King's Justice**.

        g.   **King's Court** (court of the King's bench) - established 1178. Decision of King's Courts through later centuries was the basis for English Common Law.

C.   American **Colonial Courts**

    1.   The **colonial period** spans the years from the establishment of Jamestown, Virginia (1607) to the signing of the Declaration of Independence (1776).

    2.   The **idea of courts** appeared soon after Pilgrims landed in the Mayflower (1620). A system of county courts existed in Virginia within 3 decades after 1607.

    3.   Colonial courts shaped by **3 influences**:

        a.   English **Common Law** tradition

        b.   Physical and social **environment** of North America

        c.   **Religious Beliefs** - Puritans, Quakers, and others.

    4.   The Salem (Massachusetts) **witch trials** (1691-1692) provide an example of how courts can function to restore social order in response to a threat. This is a **consensus theory** idea.

    5.   In New England colonies, minor offenses were heard in **county courts**, before justices of the peace. Serious offenses heard in the **highest court** of the colony, or in special **courts of oyer and terminer** ("hear and conclude").

    6.   As colonies became more populated and complex, **superior courts** were established to hear civil and criminal cases.

III.   *The Structure of American Courts*

Courts have **jurisdiction** over a case if it has the right to hear that case and render a decision.

        a.   **Geographical** jurisdiction - geographical area a court covers

        b.   **Subject-Matter** jurisdiction - types of cases a court may hear

        c.   **Hierarchical** jurisdiction - lower court, trial court, appeals court

        d.   **Original** jurisdiction - determines in which court a case will first be heard

America has a **dual court structure**, consisting of federal and state courts. Since there are 50 states, there are **actually 51 separate court systems** in the U.S.

A.   **Federal Courts**

    1.   There are **2 types** of federal courts:

        a.   **Constitutional courts** were created under Article III of the U.S. Constitution (Supreme Court, Courts of Appeals, District Courts).

        b.   **Legislative courts** were created by Congress to meet a certain need (U.S. Court of Military Appeals, Territorial courts, and others).

    2.   **History of the Federal Courts** - 5 stages:

        a.   Period of **Formation** (1787-1865) - years between adoption of U.S. Constitution and the end of the Civil War. The **Judiciary Act of 1789** created the Supreme Court, 13 district courts, and 3 regional circuits.

        b.   Rise in **Professionalism** (1865-1905) - move away from part-time colonial courts to permanent staff of trained jurists. **Circuit Courts of Appeals** were created in 1891.

        c.   Period of **Rational Administration** (1906-1937) - Efforts to increase efficiency of federal courts.

        d.   Increased **Bureaucratization** (1938-1966) - The Administrative Office of the U.S. Courts was created in 1939.

        e.   Era of **Technocratic Administration** (1967-present) - The Federal Judicial Center was created to conduct research on federal courts and to provide training. This emphasized central national control of the federal courts.

    3.   **The United States Supreme Court** -

        a.   The nation's court of last resort (decisions cannot be appealed).

b.   Supreme Court hears only a small fraction of cases that come before it.

c.   The Court's ruling in **Marbury v. Madison** (1803) established the doctrine of **judicial review**, that the Supreme Court can declare acts of Congress to be unconstitutional, and therefore void.

d.   **History of the Supreme Court** spans 3 periods:

    1.   1801-1865: Focus on **clarifying relationships** between the Court and the states.

    2.   1865-1937: Focus on **economic issues**.

    3.   1937-present: Focus on **civil liberties**.

4.   **U.S. Circuit Courts of Appeals -**

a.   There are **12 Circuit Courts of Appeals** that have geographic jurisdiction, plus the U.S. Court of Appeals for the Federal Circuit (in Washington, D.C.).

b.   The **intermediate appellate courts** of the federal judicial system.

c.   Most cases are heard by a **3-judge panel**. Sometimes cases are heard by all judges in the circuit, sitting **en banc**.

5.   **U.S. District Courts -**

a.   The 94 U.S. District Courts have been called the "**workhorses** of the federal judiciary."

b.   They are the **primary trial courts** of the federal system.

c.   Have **jurisdiction** over cases involving violations of federal law.

d.   **Functions** of U.S. District Courts include (Carp and Stidham):

    1.   **Norm (law) enforcement** - Acting as trial courts.

    2.   **Policy making** - Making rulings that have implications beyond a particular case. Example: prison inmate rights and prison conditions.

B. **State Courts** - Vary in each of the 50 states, but there are **three types of state courts**:

   1. **Courts of Limited Jurisdiction** - lower courts. Hear less serious cases. Example is justice of the peace court.

   2. **Courts of General Jurisdiction** - trial courts.

   3. **Appellate Courts** - Hear appeals from cases originating in the trial courts.

      a. **Intermediate appellate courts** are the middle-level appeals courts.

      b. **Court of last resort** is the highest appeals court in a particular state.

C. **Other Courts**

   1. **The Military Court-Martial -**

      a. **Primary goal** is to uphold military discipline. Law is the **Uniform Code of Military Justice**. Conviction rates are high.

      b. **General court-martial** consists of a military judge and five military jurors. Hears wide variety of cases.

      c. **Special court-martial** dispenses less serious punishments than general court-martial.

      d. **Summary court-martial** is held before a single officer, in cases of enlisted personnel charged with minor offenses.

      e. Certain court-martial decisions may be appealed to the **courts of military review** and/or the **U.S. Court of Military Appeals** in Washington, D.C.

   2. **Native Americans and the Courts**

      a. **Very complex area of law** because of many types of agreements and many courts that have jurisdiction over "Indian country" (a legal term).

      b. **Traditional Courts** are not true courts. Informal forums headed by tribal chiefs.

      c.   **Courts of Indian Offenses (CFR courts)** - Created in 1883 to dispense justice on reservations. Called CFR courts after the Code of Federal Regulations. Dominated by reservation Indian agents. These have been replaced on most reservations by...

      d.   **Tribal Courts** - Created under 1934 Indian Reorganization Act, which encouraged tribes to create their own governments and courts. Hear civil and lesser criminal cases. Judges are influential tribal leaders.

      e.   Serious offenses on Indian reservations are adjudicated in **U.S. District courts**.

   3.   **Courts of International Law** - International law governs relations between nations. Hindered by lack of enforcement body.

      a.   **International Court of Justice (World Court)**. Meets in The Hague (Netherlands). Does not usually deal with criminal matters.

      b.   In 1994, the United Nations created two temporary criminal tribunals to hear cases of genocide and war crimes, the **International Criminal Tribunal for the Former Yugoslavia** and the **International Criminal Tribunal for Rwanda**.

      c.   Many persons have called for creation of a **permanent international criminal court**. Political disputes have hindered this process.

IV.   *Administration and Reform*

   A.   **The Judiciary (Judges)** - Most powerful and visible member of the courtroom work group.

     1.   Judges **must be lawyers** in all but the lowest courts.

     2.   Judges selected by:

      a.   **Partisan elections** - appear on ballot of a political party.

      b.   **Nonpartisan elections** - party plays a role only behind the scenes.

           c.   **Merit selection -** Judicial nominating commission recommends slate of candidates to the state governor. Judges sometimes required to run in **retention elections** to keep their posts.

           d.   **Executive appointment -** Appointment by state governor alone.

           e.   **Legislative appointment -** Appointment by state legislature.

    3.   Most lawyers and judges are **men**.

    4.   1991 Senate hearings on the **nomination of Judge Clarence Thomas** to the U.S. Supreme Court illustrate political influences on courts.

B.   **Court Administration**

    1.   Courts are **complex organizations** that must be administered.

    2.   **Chief Judges** oversee administration of courts in their jurisdiction. Usually the most senior judge who has not yet reached a certain age.

    3.   **Court Clerks** oversee routine court management in many areas. They are often elected, which causes political tension. They are sometimes poorly qualified.

    4.   **Court Administrators** are trained professional managers.

    5.   The **Judicial Conference of the United States** (judges) and the **Administrative Office of the U.S. Courts** provide for more efficient management of federal courts.

C.   **Structural Reform of Courts**

    1.   Many states have adopted a **unified court system** to make administration of state courts more efficient and effective.

    2.   In 1974, Congress passed the **Speedy Trial Act**, which requires that trials in federal courts begin no later than 90 days after a suspect's indictment.

Key Terms

appellate court
Common Law
court administrator

court clerk
court of Indian offenses (CFR Court)
court of last resort
court-martial
court of general jurisdiction
court of limited jurisdiction
dual court system
intermediate appellate courts
judicial review
justice of the peace
speedy trial act
Tribal Court
U.S. circuit courts of appeals
U.S. district courts
U.S. Supreme Court

Questions for Study

1. What are some functions of courts? In other words, what good things do courts do for society as a whole? How are courts influenced by matters of power and politics?

2. Discuss some examples of courts in ancient societies. In what ways were they different from courts found in the modern United States?

3. Why is the history of English courts important for understanding the development of courts in the United States? In what ways did early English courts influence judicial structure and process in the American colonies and in the new nation?

4. What is meant by the term "dual court system?" What courts make up the dual court system?

5. Describe the structure of the federal courts, and the structure of a typical state court system.

6. What makes the United States Supreme Court a unique component of the American judicial structure? What is the source of its unique power?

7. What are some problems facing today's courts? How are these problems being addressed?

Selected Readings

Henry J. Abraham, The Judicial Process, 6th ed. (New York: Oxford University Press, 1993). A readable introduction to courts in England, the United States, and France.

James Eisenstein, Roy B. Fleming, and Peter F. Nardulli, The Contours of Justice: Communities and Their Courts (Boston, MA: Little, Brown, 1988). A sophisticated study of courts in nine American communities, from a social scientific point of view.

Alan Harding, A Social History of English Law (London: Penguin, 1966). Harding traces the development of English law from ancient times through the 19th century.

Bernard Schwartz, A History of the Supreme Court (New York: Oxford University Press, 1993). A useful chronological treatment of this singularly important American court.

Christopher E. Smith, Courts and the Poor (Chicago: Nelson-Hall, 1991). Smith examines social scientific research on the relationship between the courts and the poor, with particular emphasis on "wealth discrimination."

Ralph S. Want, ed., Want's Federal-State Court Directory (Washington, D.C.: WANT Publishing Company). This annual directory provides a concise summary of the structure of federal andstate courts, with helpful diagrams, names and addresses of each. The court structure of Canada is profiled as well.

Bob Woodward and Scott Armstrong, The Brethren: Inside the Supreme Court (New York: Simon and Schuster, 1979). An informative and interesting journalistic look into the hidden world of the nation's highest court.

Sample Test Questions

Multiple Choice Questions

1. The United States has a _____ court system.
    a. unitary
    b. dual
    c. tripartite
    d. statutory

2.   A _____ is an administrative official who performs the routine daily tasks that must be completed in order for the work of the court to be carried out.
   a.   judge
   b.   court clerk
   c.   bailiff
   d.   marshall

3.   The highest appeals court in a state government, or in the federal government, is known as a(n) _____.
   a.   intermediate appeals court
   b.   superior court
   c.   court of last resort
   d.   court of *oyer and terminer*

4.   A military trial is known as a(n) _____.
   a.   court-martial
   b.   discharge
   c.   article 22 hearing
   d.   board of military review

5.   Courts that have primary responsibility for conducting trials are known as _____.
   a.   courts of limited jurisdiction
   b.   lower courts
   c.   courts of general jurisdiction
   d.   intermediate appeals courts

6.   Candidates for the post of U.S. supreme court justice are nominated by _____.
   a.   the senate
   b.   the house of representatives
   c.   the department of justice
   d.   the president

7.   Serious criminal cases that arise on Indian reservations are usually heard in _____.
   a.   state court
   b.   federal court
   c.   the World Court
   d.   (none of the above)

8.   The United States Supreme Court consists of _____ Associate Justices and a Chief Justice.
      a.   6
      b.   7
      c.   8
      d.   9

9.   Lower courts are also known as _____.
      a.   courts of limited jurisdiction
      b.   courts of general jurisdiction
      c.   appeals courts
      d.   trial courts

10.   In the federal judicial system, trials are held in _____.
      a.   U.S. district courts
      b.   U.S. circuit courts of appeals
      c.   the U.S. Supreme Court
      d.   (all of the above)

True/False Questions

T F 11.   According to the text, one of the functions of courts is to act as agents of social change.

T F 12.   Courts are the oldest criminal justice structures, existing before police and prisons/jails.

T F 13.   The office of justice of the peace was created in England in the 14th century.

T F 14.   There are two types of federal courts. Constitutional courts, such as the U.S. Court of Military Appeals, were created by Congress to meet a certain need.

T F 15.   Traditionally, the World Court has not dealt with international matters of a criminal nature.

Essay Questions

16.   Discuss criminal courts from the points of view of consensus theory and conflict theory. That is, discuss the functions of courts (consensus theory) and the ways that courts protect the interests of the powerful (conflict theory).

17.   Detail the structure of American state and federal courts. How do the responsbilities of courts vary at different levels?

18.   In what ways have American courts been influenced by court practices in old England?

19.   How, and by whom, is court administration carried out?

20.   Discuss the various ideas that have been proposed as ways of reforming America's courts.

Answers to Sample Test Questions

1b,2b, 3c, 4a, 5c, 6d, 7b, 8c, 9a, 10a, 11T, 12T, 13T, 14F, 15T

CHAPTER EIGHT
COURTROOM ACTORS AND THE CRIMINAL TRIAL

Learning Objectives

After completing this chapter, you should understand the following topics:

1. The role of the judge, prosecutor, defense attorney, and jury.

2. Why the judge, prosecutor, and defense attorney have been referred to as the "courtroom work group."

3. Ways in which the courtroom resembles a battlefield.

4. The functions of bail, and how pretrial procedures determine which evidence may be presented at trial.

5. Stages of the trial process, from jury selection through announcement of the verdict.

6. The importance of plea bargaining to the judicial process.

7. Due process rights possessed by criminal suspects at trial.

Chapter Summary

1. Judges are responsible for managing the courtroom process. They supervise plea negotiations, conduct trials, and watch for potential errors which may provide grounds for appeal.

2. Prosecutors are attorneys who represent the state. They are key actors in the courtroom drama, possessing a great deal of discretion over whether to charge suspects, what the charges should be, what concessions may be offered in plea negotiations, and sentencing options.

3. The defense attorney represents the accused in plea negotiations and at trial. Suspects who cannot afford to hire a private attorney must be provided with one free of charge in serious cases.

4. The jury is a silent participant in criminal trials. Its members are charged with objectively examining the law and the facts of the case in order to determine whether the suspects is guilty or not guilty. If they wish, juries may disregard the

evidence and find defendants not guilty even if they believe that the suspect is in fact guilty as charged. This practice is called jury nullification.

5. Other persons who play important roles in criminal trial proceedings include court clerks, bailiffs, marshals, court reporters, probation officers, coroners, forensic technicians, expert witnesses, and police officers. Crime victims and their families play a limited role.

6. Consensus theory is consistent with the view of the courtroom as a bureaucratic organization. Within this organization, judges, prosecutors, and defense attorneys form a courtroom work group whose members cooperate to carry out the goals of the court. Conflict theory implies that the courtroom is a battleground of opposing interests.

7. Although the right to a trial is fundamental to the American system of justice, relatively few cases are resolved through trial. About 89 percent of criminal cases in state court are resolved through plea bargaining, and 92 percent in federal court.

8. American law guarantees each criminal suspect a fair trial, where their Constitutional rights are protected.

Chapter Outline

Introduction

The work of the criminal court is accomplished by people who perform their **occupational roles**, much like actors in a play.

I.   Courtroom Actors

A. **The Judge** is responsible for **overseeing** courtroom proceedings.

1. Judges are expected to be **independent mediators**, and to treat each side exactly the same.

2. Judges perform their work in the courtroom, but also **behind the scenes** in an informal manner.

3. The U.S. Constitution contains several provisions designed to **protect the independence** of federal judges:

a. Courts are **responsible only for judicial work**, not for legislation or enforcement.

b. Federal judges are appointed for **life terms**.

c. The salaries of federal judges **cannot be reduced**.

4. Federal judges are nearly always **experienced lawyers** who have political connections.

5. Most judges are white, Anglo-Saxon, Protestant **(WASP) males**.

B. **The Prosecutor** is the people's representative in criminal court.

1. The prosecutor's role includes **legal, bureaucratic**, and **political** components.

2. According to some observers, prosecutors wield more **power over the lives of others** than anyone else in America.

3. One of the key decisions made by prosecutors is the **decision to charge** a suspect with a criminal offense.

4. Prosecutors generally **pursue cases** where the evidence is strong and the case appears "winnable."

C. **Defense Counsel** represent the defendant in court.

1. **Retained counsel** is an attorney chosen and paid for by the defendant.

2. **Court-appointed counsel** are provided by the court to defendants who are unable to retain a private attorney.

   a. **Public Defenders** are paid by the state to defend criminal suspects on a full-time basis.

   b. **Assigned Counsel** are appointed by the judge from a list of local attorneys.

   c. **Contract Systems** provide attorneys who contract with the government to provide criminal defense services.

3. McIntyre's research suggests that defense attorneys view the **guilt or innocence** of their clients as irrelevant to their jobs.

D.   **The Jury -**

    1.   The **right to trial by jury** is protected by the Constitution.

    2.   Most cases are resolved not by trial but by **plea bargain** agreement.

    3.   Prospective jurors are questioned during the **voir dire** process.

        a.   Attorneys may **challenge for cause** prospective jurors who are not qualified to serve.

        b.   Attorneys may issue a certain number of **peremptory challenges**, which allow them to strike a prospective juror from the panel without stating a reason for the challenge.

E.   **Other Courtroom Actors** include court clerks, bailiffs, marshals, court reporters, probation officers, parole officers, coroners, forensic technicians, expert witnesses, police, visitors in the gallery, victims, and families of victims.

II.   *Models of the Courtroom Process*

A.   **The Courtroom Work Group Model** focuses on ways that the judge, prosecutor, and defense attorney work together to produce justice, which benefits society as a whole. This idea is consistent with **consensus theory**.

B.   **The Courtroom-as-Battleground Model** emphasizes that courts operate according to the **adversary** system. This is consistent with the **conflict approach**.

III.   *Bail and Pretrial Procedures*

A.   **Bail (pretrial release)** allows the release of a suspect upon payment of a sum of money.

    1.   The 8th Amendment prohibits **excessive bail.**

    2.   **Preventive detention** involves keeping potentially dangerous suspects in jail by denying them bail. However, methods of **predicting dangerousness** are not very accurate.

B.   **Pre-Trial Procedures -**

    1.   **Motion for discovery** - A defense motion requesting to all evidence that the prosecution will present at trial.

2.   **Motion to suppress** - A defense motion requesting the judge to prevent certain evidence from being presented by the prosecution. The **exclusionary rule** states that evidence that has been illegally seized cannot be used in court.

IV.   *The Trial and Appeals*

The case of John Hinckley, who shot President Ronald Reagan in 1981, illustrates that all **Americans are entitled to a fair trial** under the law. (consensus theory).

Most cases **do not go to trial** at all. They are resolved by plea bargain agreement.

Criminal trials typically involve the following steps:

A.   **Jury Selection** - Many lawyers believe that cases can be won or lost at this stage, by choosing the right jury.

B.   **Preliminary Instructions to the Jury** - The judge informs the jury members how to carry out their duties.

C.   **Opening Statements** - The prosecutor and defense attorney tell the jury what they believe the evidence will show in their favor.

D.   **Presentation of the Prosecution's Case** - The prosecution presents evidence and witness testimony in an attempt to convince the jury that the defendant is guilty.

E.   **Presentation of the Defense Case** - The defense presents evidence and witness testimony in an attempt to convince the jury that the defendant is not guilty.

F.   **Presentation of Rebuttal Evidence** - Prosecution and defense are offered a final opportunity to discredit evidence presented by the other side.

G.   **Closing Arguments (Summation)** - A final attempt to convince the jury.

H.   **Judge's Instructions to the Jury** - Concerning the legal issues of the case, and types of verdicts that the jury is permitted to return.

I.   **Jury Deliberation and Announcement of the Verdict** - Jury deliberations are secret, and no record is made of them. When a verdict is reached, it is announced in court.

J.   **Appeals and Post Conviction Remedies -**

    a.   **Appeals** are claims that an **error of law** occurred during the trial, which makes the results invalid.

    b.   **Postconviction remedies** are technically not appeals, because they are not limited to matters that occurred during the trial. Most common postconviction remedy is a **petition for habeas corpus relief**, which alleges that a prisoner is being held improperly.

V.   *Issues in the Adjudication Process*

A.   **Plea Bargaining** has become an accepted part of American justice.

    a.   The **consensus approach** suggests that plea bargaining benefits all parties concerned.

    b.   The **conflict approach** cautions us to watch for duress, and ways that plea bargaining may benefit some groups (judges, attorneys) at the expense of others (defendants, victims).

B.   **Rights of Suspects during Trial** - Rights are individual liberties **protected by law**.

    1.   **Right to a Jury Trial** - Jury panels must not systematically exclude any group such as women, minorities, the poor, and others.

    2.   **Right to a Speedy Trial** - Trial must be held relatively soon after a suspect is charged.

    3.   **Right to a Fair and Public Trial** - To be fair, trials must be open to the general public and the news media.

    4.   **Right to Counsel** - The Supreme Court has ruled (*Gideon v. Wainwright*, 1963) that poor persons, charged with a serious offense, who cannot afford a lawyer must be provided with one by the state.

    5.   **The Privilege Against Self-Incrimination** - Prohibits police from extracting confessions from suspects through **torture**. Allows suspects to **remain silent** in the face of questioning by police.

6.   **Right to be Protected Against Double Jeopardy** - A person **cannot be** put on trial twice for the same offense in the same jurisdiction, **if the** original trial was successfully completed (a verdict was **reached).**

7.   **Right to Confront Witnesses** - Prosecution cannot be based **solely** on the testimony of anonymous informers.

8.   **Right to the "Beyond a Reasonable Doubt" Standard** - **A higher** standard than the "preponderance of the evidence" standard **used in civil** proceedings. Each jury member must interpret what reasonable **doubt** means to him or her.

Key Terms

bail
challenge for cause
courtroom work group model
courtroom-as-battleground model
cross-examination
defense attorney
direct examination
exclusionary rule
hung jury
judge
jury nullification
motion to suppress
motion for discovery
peremptory challenge
plea bargain
post-conviction remedies
prosecutor
public defender
shield laws
voir dire

Questions for Study

1.   How are judges selected for their posts? What qualifications must they **meet?** How might judicial selection be explained by the consensus and conflict **perspectives?**

2.   What is the courtroom work group? In what ways is the courtroom **like a** battlefield?

3.   What is bail? What matters are usually brought up and resolved in pretrial procedures?

4.   List and define the typical steps involved in the trial process.

5.   What is jury nullification? Do you think that juries in criminal trials should be able to exercise this power? Why or why not?

6.   What advantages does plea bargaining provide for defendants, for the prosecution, and for the judge? What are some concerns that have been raised about the practice?

7.   Explain the most important constitutional rights that criminal suspects possess during trial.

Selected Readings

Stephen J. Adler, <u>The Jury: Disorder in the Courts</u> (New York: Doubleday, 1995). Journalist and lawyer Stephen Adler critically examines the jury, based on interviews with judges, lawyers, and former jurors.

David J. Bodenhamer, <u>Fair Trial: Rights of the Accused in American History</u> (New York: Oxford University Press, 1992). Bodenhamer traces the evolution of criminal suspects' due process rights, from the Colonial era through the 20th Century.

Alan M. Dershowitz, <u>Reasonable Doubts: The O.J. Simpson Case and the Criminal Justice System</u> (New York: Simon & Schuster, 1996). A spirited critique of the Simpson trial, by a Harvard Law School professor and member of Simpson's defense team.

Hiroshi Jukurai, Edgar W. Butler, and Richard Krooth, <u>Race and the Jury</u> (New York: Plenum, 1993). A comprehensive review of how race influences jury selection and decision-making in American criminal trials.

Lisa J. McIntyre, <u>The Public Defender: The Practice of Law in the Shadows of Repute</u> (Chicago: University of Chicago Press, 1988). In studying the public defenders of Cook County (Chicago), Illinois, McIntyre gains considerable insight into those who play this sometimes-maligned occupational role.

Peter F. Nardulli, James Eisenstein and Roy B. Flemming, <u>The Tenor of Justice</u> (Urbana, IL: University of Illinois Press, 1988). This book combines a theoretical analysis of the courtroom organization with an empirical study of 9 felony courts. Focuses on the social organization of courts, and the plea bargaining process.

Janice Shuetz, <u>The Logic of Women on Trial: Case Studies of Popular American Trials</u> (Carbondale, IL: Southern Illinois University Press, 1994). An analysis of nine important felony trials involving women defendants, from the Salem witch trials to those of Lizzie Borden, Ethel Rosenberg, Patty Hearst, Jean Harris and others.

Sample Test Questions

Multiple Choice Questions

1. Under the doctrine of _____, jurors may vote to acquit a defendant even if they believe him or her to be guilty as charged.
   a. equal justice
   b. jury nullification
   c. jury sovereignty
   d. community will

2. About _____ percent of prosecutors are women.
   a. 30
   b. 50
   c. 70
   d. 90

3. The 8th Amendment to the Constitution _____.
   a. contains the right to a trial by jury
   b. prohibits excessive bail
   c. prohibits unreasonable search and seizure
   d. requires police to obtain a warrant

4. When a defendant pleads guilty, he or she gives up the right to _____.
   a. a trial
   b. confront witnesses
   c. remain silent
   d. (all of the above)

5. The questioning of a witness by an attorney for the side that called the witness is known as _____.
   a. cross-examination
   b. direct examination
   c. redirect
   d. recross

6. Legal statutes allowing special procedures to be used for child witnesses, such as placing a screen between the child and the suspect, are known as _____.
    a. anonymity laws
    b. confidentiality laws
    c. shield laws
    d. child protective statutes

7. _____ are requests by convicted offenders that their cases be reviewed by an appeals court. They are not limited to matters about which the defense attorney objected at trial. An example is a request for a writ of *habeas corpus*.
    a. Postconviction remedies
    b. Appeals
    c. Prisoner correspondence
    d. Request for a writ of certiorari

8. A defense attorney who is employed by the government to represent criminal defendants who are too poor to afford a private attorney is a(n) _____.
    a. assigned counsel
    b. contract counsel
    c. public defender
    d. legal defender

9. Mistrials may be declared for which of the following reasons?
    a. illness or death of one of the attorneys
    b. jury tampering
    c. a hung jury
    d. (all of the above)

10. Appeals courts of last resort are responsible for reviewing _____.
    a. issues of fact
    b. issues of law
    c. jury verdicts
    d. matters of guilt or innocence

True/False Questions

T F 11. Judges, except for justices of the peace, are nearly always experienced lawyers.

T F 12. Most criminal cases in state and federal court are resolved through plea bargain rather than by a trial.

T F 13. Prosecutors are legally required to prosecute every case that is presented to them by the police.

T F 14.   Attorneys may request that prospective jurors be stricken from the jury panel if they state to the judge that the juror is unqualified to serve because of some particular reason. This is known as a peremptory challenge.

T F 15.   Jury members may legally vote for conviction if they believe that the "preponderance of the evidence" indicates the defendant's guilt.

Essay Questions

16.   Discuss the role of the judge in the courtroom process.

17.   The courtroom has been described as a battlefield. On the other hand, the courtroom actors have been described as a "courtroom work group." Compare and contrast these two models.

18.   Describe the role of the jury in the trial process. Are jurors unbiased? Should they be unbiased or should they reflect the (possibly biased) will of the community? What is jury nullification?

19.   Describe the typical stages of the trial process, from jury selection to announcement of the verdict.

20.   What due process rights are possessed by criminal suspects at trial?

Answers to Sample Test Questions

1b, 2a, 3b, 4d, 5b, 6c, 7a, 8c, 9d, 10b, 11T, 12T, 13F, 14F, 15F

CHAPTER NINE
SENTENCING

Learning Objectives

After completing this chapter, you should understand the following topics:

1. The concepts of punishment and sentencing.

2. Consensus theory and conflict theory views of punishment.

3. Philosophical justifications for punishment: the retributive and utilitarian theories.

4. Goals of sentencing, including justice, deterrence, rehabilitation, incapacitation, expression of community outrage, and restitution.

5. Types of sentences that are administered in the United States, including imprisonment, probation, intermediate punishments, and the death penalty.

6. The sentencing process, which includes activities of the court and influences from "upstream" and "downstream."

7. Reasons for sentencing reform, and methods that have been tried in order to achieve it.

8. How sentencing guidelines have changed American criminal justice.

Chapter Summary

1. Through sentencing, society punishes offenders for violations of the criminal law.

2. Consensus theory suggests that punishment is society's response to attacks on shared norms and values. Conflict theory views punishment as an effort by powerful groups to protect their interests.

3. Two other theories look at philosophical justifications of punishment. Retributive theory states that punishment is necessary to achieve justice, while Utilitarian theory believes that punishment produces beneficial outcomes for society.

4. Goals of sentencing include justice, deterrence, rehabilitation, incapacitation, expression of public outrage, and restitution.

5. In the United States, offenders may be sentenced to four types of punishment: probation, intermediate punishments, imprisonment, or death.

6.   The sentencing process involves the judge and jury, along with other influences from "upstream" and "downstream."

7.   There is some evidence that women receive different sentences than men for the same crimes. The possibility of racially biased sentencing is also a concern, especially in relation to the disproportionate number of black and Hispanic males under correctional supervision.

8.   To reduce disparity, a number of sentencing reforms have been tried. The most successful approach has been sentencing guidelines.

Chapter Outline

Introduction

A.   **Punishment** is doing something to a person in response to a wrong that the person is believed to have committed.

B.   **Sentencing** is determining and applying punishments in response to violations of the criminal law.

I.   Punishment and Sentencing

According to David Garland, punishment can be **viewed in many ways**:

a.   a **coercive relationship** between state and offender

b.   a **legal procedure**

c.   a form of **power**

d.   an instrument of **class domination**

e.   an expression of **collective feeling**

f.   a **moral action**

g.   a **ritual** event

h.   an embodiment of a certain **sensibility**

A.   **Theories of Punishment**

1.   **Consensus Theory** (Durkheim) - Crime attacks the moral consensus (collective conscience) and constitutes a threat to society.

   a.   Punishment **restores damage** done to the social order.

   b.   **Rituals** are important as symbolic reassertions of the moral authority of the group.

2.   **Conflict Theory**: The Legacy of Karl Marx

   a.   Punishment not only controls crime, but it exists partly to **protect the interests of the powerful** by keeping the lower classes in a subordinate position.

   b.   Exemplified by Reiman's admonition that "**the rich get richer and the poor get prison**."

3.   **Philosophical Justifications** - What gives society the right to punish?

   a.   **Retributive theory** argues that offenders should be punishment because **justice requires it**. Laws must be enforced if they **are to** remain meaningful. (Hegel, Kant, Aquinas, Plato).

   b.   **Utilitarian theory** argues that punishment is necessary **because it** produces important benefits for society, such as prevention of further crime through deterrence. (Bentham, Beccaria).

   c.   Both of these theories are **consistent with the consensus approach** because they assume that punishment benefits all **groups** equally.

B.   **Goals of Sentencing**

1.   **Justice (retribution)** - Criminals should be punished because they **deserve** it.

2.   **Deterrence** - Punishment may prevent further crime.

   a.   **Specific deterrence** occurs when the punishment of a person **deters** that person from committing further crimes.

        b.   **General deterrence** occurs when the punishment of one person serves as an example to others, who then refrain from committing crimes.

    3.   **Rehabilitation** involve efforts to change offenders in a positive direction.

    4.   **Incapacitation** - Protecting society by incarcerating dangerous offenders.

        a.   **Collective incapacitation** involves the incarceration of large numbers of people.

        b.   **Selective incapacitation** involves imprisoning only those high-rate offenders who are responsible for committing many crimes.

        c.   **Three-strikes-and-you're-out laws** are becoming increasingly popular as a way to imprison repeat offenders.

    5.   **Expression of Community Outrage** - By doing so, the community increases its solidarity (consensus theory).

    6.   **Restitution** is compensating a victim for loss or injury.

II.   *Administration of the Sentence*

    A.   **Sentencing Types** range from mild to harsh:

        1.   **Probation** - Convicted offenders are placed under community supervision instead of being imprisoned.

        2.   **Intermediate Punishments** are so called because they exist in the intermediate space between probation and incarceration. They include:

            a.   **Fines**

            b.   **Restitution**

            c.   **Asset forfeiture**

            d.   **Community service**

            e.   **Intensive supervision probation (ISP)**

            f.   **Electronic monitoring (house arrest)**

        g.   **Shock incarceration (boot camp)**

    3.   **Incarceration** - A term in jail or prison.

    4.   **The Death Penalty** - The number of persons executed in the U.S. has been increasing in recent years.

        a.   The Supreme Court has ruled that capital punishment is **not cruel and unusual** punishment if it is administered fairly.

        b.   Research **fails to support** a hypothesized deterrent effect of capital punishment.

        c.   Opponents of the death penalty suggest that the **death-qualified jury** is unfair. Jurors must state that they are not unequivocally opposed to the death penalty.

        d.   Consensus theory suggests that capital punishment is an **expression of community values**. Conflict theory questions why most persons who are executed are **young, black, and poor**.

B.   **The Sentencing Process** (see Figure 9.3 on page 279: "The Sentencing Stream")

    1.   **Three groups** influence the sentencing process:

        a.   **Judges and Parole Boards** directly influence the type and length of sentence to be served.

        b.   **Upstream Groups** influence sentencing **before** judges and parole boards enter the picture. State legislatures and the U.S. Congress, probation officials, attorneys for the prosecution and defense.

        c.   **Downstream factors** influence sentencing **after** judges and parole boards. Prison good time policies, parole, revocation of probation or parole, and escape valve laws.

III.   *Continuing Controversies*

A.   **Sentencing and Women** - Women account for about 15 percent of persons convicted of felony offenses in state courts, and 1 percent of those executed each year.

B. **Sanctions for Corporate Crime** - The low rate of prosecutions of corporation illustrates conflict theory's prediction that the law will tend to protect the powerful.

C. **Sentencing Reform and Sentencing Guidelines**

1. **Sentencing Disparity** is the imposition of widely varying sentences on persons convicted of similar crimes.

2. **Reforms** aim to reduce sentencing disparity. Many methods have been tried:

a. Parole Guidelines -

b. Voluntary Sentencing Guidelines -

c. Statutory Determinate Sentencing -

d. Sentencing Guidelines Created by Sentencing Commissions -

e. Presumptive Sentencing -

f. Mandatory Sentencing -

g. Enhanced Sentencing Review at the Appellate Level -

3. The most effective sentencing reform has been **Sentencing Guidelines Created by Sentencing Commissions**. This method has gained widespread support and has been enacted into law by the federal government and many state governments.

D. **Racial Bias** - Studies have shown that the federal sentencing guidelines, implemented in 1989, have led to **bias against blacks** in the federal courts. **Blacks** receive sentences that are 41 percent longer than white defendants. Over 1/4 of all black adults can expect to be imprisoned in a state or federal prison during their lifetimes. These findings **support conflict theory**.

Key Terms

asset forfeiture
bifurcated trial
brutalization hypothesis
capital punishment

collective conscience (Durkheim)
determinate sentencing
deterrence, general
deterrence, specific
escape valve laws
good time credits
incapacitation, selective
incapacitation, collective
indeterminate sentencing
intermediate punishments
plea bargain
presumptive sentencing guidelines
probation
punishment
rehabilitation
restitution
retribution (justice)
retributive theory of punishment
utilitarian theory of punishment
vengeance
voluntary sentencing guidelines

Questions for Study

1. What is the purpose of criminal punishment, according to consensus theory and conflict theory?

2. What answers do retributive theory and utilitarian theory give to the question "What gives society the right to punish criminal offenders?"

3. According to the text, what are some goals of criminal sentencing?

4. What types of prison and non-prison sentences are given out in the United States today?

5. What does the research evidence suggest about whether the death penalty deters others from committing similar crimes?

6. What is sentencing disparity? What strategies have been adopted by the federal government and the states in order to reform sentencing and reduce disparity?

7. How does the issue of disparate sentencing for women and blacks illustrate the conflict perspective?

Selected Readings

Dean J. Champion, <u>The U.S. Sentencing Guidelines: Implications for Criminal Justice</u> (New York: Praeger, 1989). A collection of articles on the rise of sentencing guidelines, and the impacts that they have had on police, courts, and corrections.

Antony Duff and David Garland, eds., <u>A Reader on Punishment</u> (New York: Oxford University Press, 1994). Contains insightful articles on various aspects of punishment.

Lois G. Forer, <u>A Rage to Punish</u> (New York: W. W. Norton, 1994). A critical examination of the mandatory sentencing movement, by a former judge. Forer concludes that it is a mistake to restrict the discretion of judges through mandatory sentencing policies.

Graeme Newman, <u>The Punishment Response</u> (Albany, NY: Harrow & Heston, 1985). A well written and theoretically sophisticated examination of punishment in historical and social context.

Ernest van den Haag, <u>Punishing Criminals: Concerning a Very Old and Painful Question</u> (Lanham, MD: University Press, 1991). A discussion of philosophies of punishment, and implications of current punishment methods for the control of crime.

Robert Johnson, <u>Death Work: A Study of the Modern Execution Process</u>, second edition (Pacific Grove, CA: Brooks/Cole). An examination of capital punishment in America, as it is experienced by condemned inmates and as it is managed by prison staff. The book is particularly useful for its descriptions of the effects of "death work" on both groups of participants.

William Spelman, <u>Criminal Incapacitation</u>, (New York: Plenum Press, 1994). A detailed analysis of the research bearing on costs and benefits of adopting incapacitation strategies to control crime.

Sample Test Questions

Multiple Choice Questions

1. _____ is a criminal punishment strategy in which offenders are sentenced to a specified amount of time under correctional supervision.
   a. Indeterminate sentencing
   b. Determinate sentencing
   c. Day fines
   d. Mandatory imprisonment

2. When an offender compensates a victim for injuries or loss, this is referred to as
   _____.
   a. retribution
   b. bail
   c. recognizance
   d. (none of the above)

3. The notion that executions or other violent events can cause people to engage in more violence is known as _____.
   a. the brutalization hypothesis
   b. the copy-cat hypothesis
   c. the neutralization hypothesis
   d. the violent events hypothesis

4. Under a _____ system, judges are required to hand down sentences that match a set of guidelines.
   a. voluntary sentencing guidelines
   b. presumptive sentencing guidelines
   c. parole guidelines
   d. utilitarian sentencing guidelines

5. What does research suggest about the possible deterrent effect of capital punishment?
   a. Most research fails to support a deterrent effect.
   b. Most research finds that a deterrent effect exists.
   c. Research studies have not been conducted on this question.

6. Imprisoning large numbers of people without attempting to classify them into more dangerous or less dangerous categories is called _____.
   a. group imprisonment
   b. declassified imprisonment
   c. selective incapacitation
   d. collective incapacitation

7. Which of the following sanctions involves the most persons on any given day?
   a. probation
   b. prison
   c. jail
   d. parole

8. Which of the following is NOT an intermediate punishment?
   a. asset forfeiture
   b. boot camp
   c. restitution
   d. (all of the above are intermediate punishments)

9. About how many persons are legally executed in the United States each year?
   a. less than 100
   b. 100-200
   c. 201-300
   d. 301 or more

10. Legislative statutes that require a certain number of prisoners to be released before others can be let in are known as _____.
    a. front door solutions
    b. escape valve laws
    c. prisoner statutes
    d. indeterminate release laws

True/False Questions

T F 11. Studies have shown that the federal sentencing process is biased against black defendants.

T F 12. According to the text, the most effective sentencing reform strategy has been voluntary sentencing guidelines.

T F 13. Probation is an intermediate punishment.

T F 14. The **justice** goal of sentencing advocates punishment of criminals because they deserve it.

T F 15. The Supreme Court currently views the death penalty as cruel and unusual punishment, which is prohibited by the 8th Amendment.

Essay Questions

16. What is the relationship between punishment and criminal sentencing? What are some other goals of sentencing, besides punishment?

17. Discuss the concept of punishment, from the points of view of consensus theory and conflict theory.

18.   **What** are the four types of criminal sentence? Discuss each type, in relation to its goals.

19.   **What** strategies have been advocated as means of sentencing reform? Which have been most successful?

20.   **Discuss** the "sentencing stream" model. What influences the sentencing process at the various locations along the bank of the sentencing stream?

Answers to Sample Test Questions

1b, 2d, 3a, 4b, 5a, 6d, 7a, 8d, 9a, 10b, 11T, 12F, 13F, 14T, 15F

CHAPTER TEN
IMPRISONMENT: HISTORY AND STRUCTURE

Learning Objectives

After completing this chapter, you should understand the following topics:

1. The development of punishment in medieval England, colonial America, and the United States.

2. How early women's prisons reflected female gender roles.

3. What types of facilities make of the structure of American institutional corrections.

4. Differences in security levels.

5. How jails differ from state and federal prisons.

6. The functions of jails, according to the consensus and conflict perspectives.

7. Effects of the prison "building boom."

8. Privatization issues, supermax prisons, and attempts to control prison expansion.

Chapter Summary

1. American punishment methods were influenced by practices in Europe. England played a particularly important role. Early innovations in imprisonment included workhouses, houses of correction, Bridewells, hulks, gaols, and the use of ships to transport convicts to distant colonies.

2. Colonial jails were used to house suspects until trial, and for short terms of imprisonment.

3. Punishment entered an age of reform in the late 18th Century. The penitentiary combined solitary confinement with productive work in the hope that prisoners could be rehabilitated.

4. During the 19th century, America adopted the penitentiary as its preferred sanction for persons convicted of serious crimes. Prison architecture and methods of discipline were often modeled after those in use at Auburn prison in New York State. Prison farms and plantations were widely used in the South.

5.   A second wave of prison reform began in the 1870s with the opening of the Elmira Reformatory. The movement reached full flower during the Progressive Era in the first two decades of the 20th century. The rehabilitative ideal dominated American prison systems until the 1960s.

6.   Women offenders were housed in men's prisons until separate facilities were women were built. Women prisoners have always received fewer resources than their male counterparts.

7.   Prisons are operated at the state and federal levels. Jails are generally administered at the local level. Some prisons and jails are managed by private corporations.

8.   Since the 1970s, the number of prison and jail institutions has grown dramatically. Likewise, the number of prisoners under state or federal custody has increased at a faster rate than any seen during the entire 20th century. This has caused the facilities to become severely crowded. Proposed solutions to the prison population problem include front door options, back door options, side door options, and trap door options.

9.   Consensus theory suggests that imprisonment is a necessary means of dealing with the problem of crime. The conflict approach sees incarceration as one more way that powerful groups can protect their own interests at the expense of the poor and minorities.

Chapter Outline

The **Running Story in the Part 4 Opener** continues the case of Dawn Hamilton, a young girl who was murdered. In this installment of the story, students learn that DNA testing has been conducted on evidence from Kirk Bloodsworth's trial, and that the results show he cannot be linked to the evidence in the case. Bloodsworth is released from prison and awarded $300,000 from the state of Maryland. The running story illustrates the stages of the criminal justice process, and some of the issues and ambiguities surrounding criminal justice in America.

Introduction

There are now **more people in American prisons than ever before**, and there has never been a higher proportion of people under some form of correctional supervision.

I.   History of Imprisonment

    A.   **The English Influence**

1. Feudal lords built **dungeons** in their castles during the Middle Ages (500-1500 A.D.)

2. The first mention of **imprisonment** appears about 890.

3. Sheriffs used **gaols** by the 11th century. King Henry II required that each county build a gaol in 1166.

4. **Bridewells**, or houses of correction were built in England after 1565.

5. **Consensus theory** suggests that gaols and houses of corrections were created in response to the new demands of urban communities.

6. **Conflict theory** suggests that gaols were created to meet a perceived threat to established groups from beggars and outlaws, and to create a cheap labor force of prisoners.

7. **Transportation** of prisoners to English colonies began in the late 16th century.

8. **Hulks** were old ships that were used as places of imprisonment. Conditions on the hulks were dismal.

B. **The Colonial Era: 1607-1776**

1. Spans the years between the settlement of **Jamestown** to the signing of the **Declaration of Independence**, 1607-1776.

2. Punishment in the colonial period exhibited **3 distinguishing features**:

   a. **Corporal punishment** (punishment of the body). Whipping, stocks, pillory, branding, ducking stool, hanging. Sometimes offenders were banished from the community.

   b. **Public punishment**. In the town square or other public place.

   c. **Little or no use of imprisonment**. Local jails served to hold suspects for short periods until trial. No prisons for long-term confinement.

C.   **The Rise of Imprisonment: 1776-1900**

1.   The first to recommend use of imprisonment to confine and rehabilitate was the Quaker **William Penn** (1644-1718), founder of Pennsylvania.

2.   The **18th century Enlightenment** in Europe and America was a time of new ideas and questioning of established tradition.

   a.   Corporal punishment became less common.

   b.   Public punishment replaced by punishment in the prison compound.

   c.   Imprisonment became preferred method of punishment for serious crimes.

3.   In America, reformers placed their hopes in the **penitentiary**, which combined imprisonment with rehabilitation efforts.

   a.   First penitentiary in America was Philadelphia's **Walnut Street Penitentiary (1790)**, a wing of the Walnut Street Jail.

   b.   At Walnut Street Penitentiary, the program was based on solitude and hard labor.

   c.   Prisoners kept in their cells, and they were prevented from speaking with others. It was hoped that silent contemplation and reading the Bible would lead to rehabilitation of offenders.

   d.   Some scholars see the penitentiary as an American invention, but similar institutions were established in Europe nearly 200 years earlier (Amsterdam *rasphuis* and others).

1.   **The Pennsylvania and Auburn Systems**

   a.   Heated controversy between penologists in Pennsylvania and New York.

   b.   Pennsylvania system based on silence and solitary confinement in large cells, where prisoners worked alone.

   c.   Auburn officials conducted a test in 1821, when 80 criminals were kept in solitary cells without work. Many mental breakdowns and suicide attempts caused officials to cancel the test after one year.

      d.   From 1821 on, the Auburn system used small cells for sleeping at night, and prisoners together performed factory-like work during the day. As in Pennsylvania, prisoners were not permitted to speak.

      e.   The Auburn system eventually won out because it was cheaper to operate since prisoners could do factory-like work and cells were smaller. Most U.S. prisons in 19th century were built on the Auburn model.

      f.   The many large castle-like prisons built in the 19th century made imprisonment seem like the only alternative for social control. It is now hard for us to think of other means of criminal punishment.

2.   **Early Reform - Three institutions** embody early prison reform efforts:

      a.   **Walnut Street Penitentiary (1790)** - The nation's first penitentiary.

      b.   **New York House of Refuge (1825)** - Began the juvenile reform movement.

      c.   **Elmira (N.Y.) Reformatory (1876)** - Used many new methods to effect the rehabilitation of adult prisoners.

            1.   Superintendent was **Zebulon Brockway (1827-1920)**, who put into place many new rehabilitative ideas.

            2.   **Indeterminate sentences** kept prisoners behind bars until they made satisfactory progress toward rehabilitation.

            3.   **Prisoners were divided into three grades**, based on their conformity to prison rules. They performed industrial work, religious studies, physical exercise, and military drill.

      d.   Consensus theorists view the 19th century rise of the penitentiary as **progress toward reform**. Conflict theorists see the penitentiary as a means of **increasing state power** over the lower classes.

3.   **Southern Punishment and Black Americans**

      a.   In the states of the old Confederacy, criminal punishment was closely linked to the **social control of the poor black underclass**.

b. Slavery was illegal, but southern **penitentiaries and road camps** maintained domination of blacks by whites.

c. The **convict lease system** allowed business owners to use cheap labor of inmates in the convict camps. Many abuses occurred, and conditions in the camps were horrible.

d. **Chain gangs** maintained county roads.

e. Huge **prison farms (plantations)** were created near the end of the 19th century, especially in the Gulf states.

f. Border states (WV, MD, MS, VA, and KS) used **northern-style industrial prisons** built on the Auburn model.

4. In **the West**, prisons were built on the Auburn model as frontier settlements became territories, and then states.

5. **Prisons for Women -**

a. Women were first incarcerated in designated **areas of men's prisons**.

b. **Separate women's prisons** were later built.

c. The **Women's Reformatory** was a new type of institution built after 1870. Emphasized traditional female gender roles.

d. Women's prisons have always garnered **fewer resources** than men's prisons. **Consensus theory** suggests that this is because there have always been relatively few women inmates. **Conflict theory** sees this as a reflection of the power of men over women in the wider society.

6. **The Prison in the 20th Century -**

a. By the **close of the 19th century**, the prison had become firmly established as the primary means of dealing with convicted felons. But conditions were very poor.

b. During the **Progressive Era (1900-1920)**, Americans refocused their efforts on prison reform and an emphasis on rehabilitation of prisoners.

    c.   John Irwin suggests that **men's prisons passed through three phases** during the 20th century:

        1.   **The Big House prison (late 19th century - 1945)** - 19th century fortress prisons.

             a.   Stone walls and buildings, fortress architecture, cell blocks stacked three to five floors high. Noisy, drafty, oppressively hot in summer.

             b.   Guards kept strict control over inmates through threats, beatings, and solitary confinement.

             d.   Clear social norms of prisoner and guard subcultures.

        2.   **The Correctional Institution (1945 - late 1960s)**

             a.   Emphasized rehabilitation of prisoners through scientific treatment.

             b.   Social upheavals of 1960s (Vietnam War, riots in cities, assassinations) combined with demise of rehabilitative ideal.

        3.   **The Violent Contemporary Prison (late 1960s - present)**

             a.   A place of hate, violence, racial divisions, and gang warfare.

             b.   The equivalent of an urban ghetto.

II.   ***American Prisons and Jails***

Organized according to:

Jurisdiction - the level of government that maintains the facility (federal, state, local).

Security Level - the level of control within the facility, and the extent of architectural features (fences, walls, gates) that maintain control.

A.   **The Federal Prison System** - The U. S. Bureau of Prisons

     1.   **United States Penitentiaries** - maximum security

     2.   **Federal Correctional Institutions** - medium security or low security

     3.   **Metropolitan Correctional Centers** - federal jails

     4.   **Federal Prison Camps** - minimum security

     5.   **Satellite Camps** - minimum security camps located near larger facilities

B.   **State Prisons** - Each state operates its own prison system.

     1.   **Maximum security prisons**

     2.   **Medium security prisons**

     3.   **Minimum Security prisons**

     4.   A new type of facility is the **Supermax prison**, designed to keep the most dangerous inmates in solitary confinement.

C.   **Jails**

     1.   Administered at the **local level**, usually by counties.

     2.   **Hold a broad mix** of sentenced and unsentenced inmates.

          a.   suspects who have not been convicted of an offense but who are waiting for a hearing or trial

          b.   convicted offenders who have not yet been sentenced

          c.   serious offenders being held for transfer to state prison

          d.   prisoner who would normally be in state prison but who are serving their terms in local jail because there is no room for them in state prison

          e.   parole violators and probation violators

3. Located **close to courts**, often in urban areas.

4. Ronald Goldfarb calls jails "**the ultimate ghetto** of the criminal justice system"

5. John Irwin adopts a conflict perspective. He sees the jail as a place for society to manage "**the rabble**," its disreputable underclass.

III. *Issues and Problems*

A. **The Prison Building Boom -**

1. The **U.S. imprisons a higher percentage** of its citizens than any other developed nation.

2. Prison **populations began exploding** in the 1970s. By the middle 1990, the number of people in American prison had increased by a factor of 4.

3. During this period, the **incarceration rate** also increased by a factor of 4.

4. **Crowding** is a major problem in prisons.

5. **Loss of faith** in rehabilitative model, and rise of "warehousing."

6. When the number of prisoners exceeds the 6 million mark, they will **outnumber all the full-time students** in the nation's colleges and universities.

B. **Privatization -**

1. **Privatization** in corrections takes 4 forms:

   a. Contracting of prison and jail services

   b. Prison Industries

   c. Construction of prison and jail facilities

   d. Private management of prisons and jails

2. Many are **in favor** of privatization, but others **express concerns** over costs and possible violation of inmates' rights.

3.   From a **consensus perspective**, privatization may be less costly and more efficient than public management of correctional facilities. **Conflict theorists** ask whether the profit motive will result in lowered levels of service and possible abuses of inmate rights.

4.   **More research needs to be conducted** on the relative benefits and costs of privatization.

C.   **Supermax Prisons** - An old idea that has gained a new foothold.

1.   Based on the idea of **solitary confinement**.

2.   **Inmates kept in cells** nearly all day. Allowed no contact with other prisoners.

3.   Architecture designed for **ultimate security** and control.

4.   First attempt by federal government at a supermax prison was **Alcatraz**, from 1934-1963.

5.   Federal government's **newest supermax prison** (as of early 1999) is Florence, Colorado.

6.   **Many states** have recently built supermax prisons.

7.   Supermax prisons **may be safer** for inmates and staff (consensus theory), but some have been **criticized** for violating United Nations standards for the treatment of prisoners (conflict theory).

D.   **Controlling Expansion** - What can be done? Construction and operation of prisons and jails is **very expensive**, and there comes a point when this cost cuts into other governmental services such as education, social services, transportation, and infrastructure repair.

1.   **Front door options** - Send fewer offenders to prisons. Sentencing policies, prosecutorial discretion, legislation.

2.   **Back door options** - Release more prisoners into the community. Parole, shorter sentences, early release programs.

3.   **Side door options** - Resentencing programs for prisoners who are already serving their sentences.

4. **Trap door options** - Emergency release programs that release one inmate for each one who is imprisoned.

In sum, the **consensus approach** suggests that imprisonment may be necessary to maintain an orderly society. The **conflict approach** questions whether there might be other means of punishment that are less costly and that involve less deprivation for imprisoned persons.

A **fundamental question** concerning the history and structure of imprisonment is "Why do it this way rather than another way?"

Key Terms

Auburn system
bridewell
convict lease system
hulks
incarceration rate
institutional corrections
jail
maximum security
medium security
minimum security
penitentiary
Pennsylvania system
prison
privatization
security level
supermax prisons
transportation

Questions for Study

1. In what ways were the Auburn system of inmate discipline and the Pennsylvania system different? How were they similar?

2. What new approaches were utilized at the Elmira Reformatory and at reformatories for women?

3. What factors made punishment strategies in the Southern states unique?

4. What significant changes occurred in American prisons during the 20th century?

5.   How do prisons at the various security levels ("supermax," maximum security, medium security, minimum security) differ from one another?

6.   In what ways are local jails different from state and federal prisons?

7.   Why have local jails been referred to as "ghettos?" Is this term closer to the consensus or conflict view?

8.   What was the prison "building boom," and what factors caused it to occur?

Selected Readings

David Garland, Punishment and Modern Society: A Study in Social Theory (Chicago: University of Chicago Press, 1990). One of the most sophisticated theoretical treatments of punishment to date. Garland analyzes the punishment-related work of Durkheim, Weber, Marx, Rusche and Kirchheimer, and Foucault.

Blake McKelvey, American Prisons: A History of Good Intentions (Montclair, NJ: Patterson Smith, 1977). A classic historical study of the rise of imprisonment in America.

Norval Morris and David J. Rothman, eds., The Oxford History of the Prison: The Practice of Punishment in Western Society, (New York: Oxford University Press, 1998). A timely and comprehensive collection of chapters by an eminent group of scholars. Includes several interesting photographs and woodcuts.

Joel A. Thompson and G. Larry Mays, eds., American Jails: Public Policy Issues, (Chicago: Nelson-Hall, 1991). A timely collection of scholarly essays focusing on public policy issues concerning jails.

Gary W. Bowman, Simon Hakim and Paul Seidenstat, eds., Privatizing Correctional Institutions, (New Brunswick, NJ: Transaction, 1993). This reader contains articles on various aspects of privatization of correctional institutions. Contains a foreword by former Chief Justice of the Supreme Court Warren Burger.

John Irwin and James Austin, It's About Time: America's Imprisonment Binge, (Belmont, CA: Wadsworth, 1994). An analysis of imprisonment in the United States, from a conflict perspective. Irwin and Austin argue that America's excessive use of the imprisonment sanction should be curtailed.

Robert P. Weiss and Nigel South, eds., Comparing Prison Systems: Toward a Comparative and International Penology, (Amsterdam: Gordon and Breach, 1998). This edited volume compares and contrasts the prison systems of sixteen nations throughout the world, approaching them along a variety of dimensions and focusing on patterns of crisis and change over the last two decades.

Sample Test Questions

Multiple Choice Questions

1. 16th century English houses of correction were known as _____.
    a. refuges
    b. Cornwalls
    c. Bridewells
    d. hulks

2. An imprisonment facility whose architecture and daily routine place few restrictions on inmate freedom, and which is usually not surrounded by any walls or fences is called a _____.
    a. country club prison
    b. maximum security prison
    c. medium security prison
    d. minimum security prison

3. The method of prison discipline adopted in the late 18th and early 19th centuries, involving long sentences served in silent and solitary confinement was _____.
    a. the Pennsylvania system
    b. the Auburn system
    c. the Ohio system
    d. the Colorado system

4. A program that allowed business owners to submit bids for the use of convict labor, especially in the South, was _____.
    a. the convict labor system
    b. the placing out system
    c. the convict lease system
    d. the lowest bid system

5. John Irwin sees jails as a place where society manages _____.
    a. serious criminals
    b. the rabble
    c. the philistines
    d. immigrants

6.   Alcatraz prison, in San Francisco Bay, was managed by the federal government from 1934-1963. Today we would classify Alcatraz as a _____ prison.
   a.   minimum security
   b.   medium security
   c.   maximum security
   d.   supermax

7.   Methods of controlling prison expansion that focus on resentencing programs for prisoners who are already serving their sentences are known as _____.
   a.   front door options
   b.   back door options
   c.   side door options
   d.   trap door options

8.   The _____ was a type of 18th century and 19th century prison which combined imprisonment with intensive efforts to rehabilitate convicted adult offenders.
   a.   house of refuge
   b.   penitentiary
   c.   panopticon
   d.   asylum

9.   The movement to turn construction and/or management of imprisonment facilities over to profit-making companies is known as _____.
   a.   capitalism
   b.   deregulation
   c.   lateral transfer
   d.   privatization

10.   The primary factor that made punishment in the American South different from punishment in the North was _____.
   a.   greater use of industrial prisons
   b.   control of the black underclass
   c.   little or no use of chain gangs
   d.   abolition of prison farms

True/False Questions

T F 11.   In 1166, King Henry II required that each county in England construct a gaol.

T F 12.   According to the conflict perspective, gaols were constructed in old England in part to meet a perceived threat to established groups from beggars and outlaws.

T F 13.   During the American colonial period, punishment was often carried out in public.

T F 14.   The first penitentiary in America was the New York House of Refuge.

T F 15.   The type of prison that John Irwin calls "the correctional facility" was known for its emphasis on rehabilitation of prisoners.

Essay Questions

16.   Detail the structure of institutional corrections in America, at both the federal and state levels.

17.   Discuss the American jail, from a consensus perspective and a conflict perspective. What functions do jails perform (consensus theory) and how do jails further the interests of the powerful (conflict theory)?

18.   Imprisonment of women has followed somewhat of a different history than imprisonment of men. Discuss these differences. How does the social structure of the womens' prison differ from the social structure of the prison for men?

19.   Detail the history of imprisonment, from its ancient origins, to old England, the American colonial era, and the 19th century.

20.   How has American imprisonment changed during the 20th century? How might these changes be interpreted from the points of views of consensus theory and conflict theory?

Answers to Sample Test Questions

1c, 2d, 3a, 4c, 5b, 6d, 7c, 8b, 9d, 10b, 11T, 12T, 13T, 14F, 15T

CHAPTER ELEVEN
LIVING AND WORKING IN PRISON: INMATES AND OFFICERS

Learning Objectives

After completing this chapter, you should understand the following topics:

1.   Characteristics of male and female prison inmates.

2.   Main assumptions of the deprivation and importation models of prisonization.

3.   How the consensus and conflict perspectives can help us to understand the social environment of the prison.

4.   How correctional treatment programs are influenced by the principle of less eligibility and the "nothing works" myth.

5.   The work environment of male and female correctional officers.

6.   The problem of individual and collective prison violence.

7.   Legal rights of prisoners.

8.   Some strategies for effective prison management and prison reform.

Chapter Summary

1.   The prison is a total institution where staff and inmates inhabit different social worlds.

2.   Theories of prisonization attempt to explain why inmate social structures arise in opposition to staff. Deprivation theory locates the cause of prisonization in the pains of imprisonment. Importation theory points to the criminal values and norms brought into the prison from the streets. These two theories closely parallel the consensus and conflict approaches.

3.   Women prisoners endure all of the hardships experienced by their male counterparts, along with problems specific to women. Treatment programs for women have traditionally been under funded and structured around stereotypical "women's" occupations.

4.   Correctional treatment programs are designed to effect some positive change in prison inmates. Treatment programs have historically encountered opposition

related to the principle of less eligibility. After a period of time in which the "nothing works" doctrine was widely held, many scholars now believe that well-run correctional treatment programs can be effective.

5.   Correctional officers perform a difficult role that combines vigilance and security with service to inmates. Women have entered the ranks of correctional officers in recent decades, but they still encounter gender-based resistance.

6.   Prisons are violent places. Violence may be individual or collective. Both inmates and officers are victims of prison violence, and violence may be initiated by members of either group. Most violence is directed by prisoners at other prisoners.

7.   After decades with no legal standing, prison inmates have had many constitutional rights affirmed by the courts.

8.   Consensus theory and conflict theory suggest that the challenge for the future is to create well-managed prisons that are effective in meeting their goals while taking into account the needs of multiple interest groups in the prison and on the outside.

Chapter Outline

Introduction

It is **important to study the prison environment** because:

1.   Nearly all prisoners will someday be **released**. We should be **aware of what** happens to them during their incarceration.

2.   We may be able to improve the **quality of work life** for correctional officers.

3.   Prisons are paid for by our **tax dollars**.

I.   The Prison Environment

A.   The prison is a **total institution** (Goffman), whose purpose is to totally control its inmates.

1.   On entering the institution, prisoners undergo a process of **mortification of the self**.

2.   The prison social environment is a **caste system** with two opposing social systems: the world of the inmates and the world of the officers.

II. *Living in Prison*

A. **Characteristics of Prisoners** -

1. U.S. **state and federal prisons** held 1.2 million offenders at year-end 1996.

2. 94 percent were **male**, and 6 percent **female**.

3. 48 percent were **white**, and 50 percent **black**.

4. 46 percent of state prisoners were serving time for a **violent offense**.

5. Recent years have seen an increase in prisoners sentenced for **drug offenses**.

B. **Theories of Prisonization** -

Prisonization (def.): The process by which inmates develop their own social norms and values, in opposition to those of prison staff.

1. The norms of the prisoner subculture are called the **inmate code**.

   a. The inmate code prohibits inmates from **informing** prison staff about each other's activities.

   b. The penalty for being an informer ("snitch") is **death** at the **hands** of other inmates.

   c. The inmate code may have **lost some of its force** in recent decades.

2. **Deprivation Theory** suggests that the inmate code is a response to harsh prison conditions. This is consistent with the consensus approach, which sees prisoner adaptations serving to meet certain needs that arise in the prison environment.

   A. **Gresham Sykes** (1958) enumerates the **pains of imprisonment**.

      1. **Deprivation of Liberty** - Represents the moral condemnation of society.

      2. **Deprivation of Goods and Services** - Makes it difficult to establish an identity based on possessions.

124

3. **Deprivation of Heterosexual Relations** - To cope, some prisoners engage in solitary sex, become sexual predators, or participate in conjugal visits (family visitation).

4. **Deprivation of autonomy** - Few adults enjoy being treated like children.

5. **Deprivation of Security** - The threat of violence is ever present in prison.

B. Professor Hans Toch's interviews with prisoners uncovered seven **focal concerns**: activity, privacy, safety, emotional feedback, support, structure, and freedom.

1. Inmates cope by finding or creating **niches**.

3. **Importation Theory** suggests that values and norms of the inmate subculture are "imported" into the prison from the street (Irwin and Cressey).

A. **Criminal identities** (Irwin and Cressey):

1. **Thief** - An established criminal identity that is developed before imprisonment.

2. **Convict** - An identity that is carved out in prison itself.

3. **Square John** - A non-criminal identity.

B. The inmate code has **lost strength** due to crowding, gangs, and violence.

C. **Women in Prison** - About 6 percent of all state and federal prisoners are women.

1. As with men, the social world of women in prison is **opposed to the staff world**.

2. But women often create **pseudo family structures** to provide a substitute for actual family relationships.

3. **Children** are a special concern for women inmates, about 76 percent of whom are mothers.

4. The **consensus approach** suggests that women's imprisonment is necessary and useful for society.

5. The **conflict approach** sees imprisonment of women as an example of domination of women by men.

D. **Death Row**

1. There were **3,219 inmates on death row** at year-end 1996.

2. **About 1 percent** of death row inmates have their sentences carried out each year.

3. In **McCleskey v. Kemp**, the Supreme Court ruled that statistical evidence of racial bias in applying the death penalty cannot be used to show bias in any particular inmate's case.

4. According to Robert Johnson, living on death row is a **psychological nightmare** for condemned inmates.

5. Correctional officers who carry out the death sentence strive to maintain **emotional distance** and to perform their work with expertise and precision.

III. *Correctional Treatment* - Programs designed to reduce the likelihood of **recidivism** (inmates committing further crime after their release from custody).

A. On first being admitted to the prison, inmates are put through a **classification process** to determine their security requirements and program needs.

B. **Types of correctional treatment programs** include:

1. **Educational** programs

2. **Vocational** programs

3. **Counseling** programs

4. **Religious** programs

5. **Recreational** programs

6. **Peer support** groups, such as Alcoholics Anonymous

7. **Service** groups, such as the Lifers Group, or the Jaycees

8. **Shock incarceration** - "boot camp" programs which usually include a drug treatment component and other treatment options

C. **Security issues** and the **principle of less eligibility** are two factors affecting correctional treatment.

1. **Security issues** must take precedence over all other prison goals.

2. **The principle of less eligibility** is the idea that prisoners should receive no better treatment than the poorest law-abiding citizens.

D. **The "Nothing Works" Myth** -

1. In 1974, an **article by Robert Martinson** and others examined treatment programs for 1945-1967 and concluded that few programs reduced recidivism.

2. In the midst of a conservative political climate, many politicians and scholars embraced the report and concluded that "**nothing works**" in correctional rehabilitation.

3. **Martinson recanted** his earlier conclusions in a later paper, which received little attention.

C. **Successful Treatment Programs** - Recent research suggests that carefully administered and targeted programs can be effective.

IV. *Working in Prison: Correctional Officers*

A. **Characteristics of Officers** -

1. **Qualifications** vary by jurisdiction.

2. Officers generally must be at least a **high school graduate, 18 years old** (sometimes 21), and be able to pass **physical and psychological tests**.

3. The job of correctional officer is **ambiguous**, combining the roles of social control agent and helping agent. This sometimes results in **role strain**.

4. Prison order is **negotiated** between officers and inmates (symbolic interactionist theory).

5. Typical **correctional officer tasks** include (Lombardo):

    a. Block officers

    b. Work detail officers

    c. Industrial shop and school officers

    d. Yard officers

    e. Administration building officers

    f. Wall officers

    g. Relief officers

6. Lombardo's research suggests that **correctional officers rank their duties** in the following order of importance: human service tasks, order maintenance, security, supervision, rule enforcement.

B. **Women as Correctional Officers -**

1. **Title VII of the Civil Rights Act of 1964** opened up previously all-male occupations to women.

2. By 1995, **19 percent** of the security staff in state and federal prisons were women.

3. Women correctional officers still **experience difficulty** from their male colleagues.

4. Like men, women become correctional officers mainly for the **pay and fringe benefits**.

V. *Issues in Correctional Management*

A. **Violence in Prison -**

1. Most violence is committed by **inmates**, but **officers** sometimes use violence also.

2. From a **consensus viewpoint**, violence can be functional for both inmates and officers.

3. From a **conflict perspective**, violence reflects the struggle between prisoners, and between prisoners and officers in the combative prison world.

4. **Collective prison violence** is called a riot. Martin and Zimmerman examined 6 models of riots:

    a. Environmental conditions model

    b. Spontaneity model

    c. Conflict model

    d. Collective behavior and social control model

    e. Power vacuum model

    f. Rising expectations/relative deprivation model

5. Social scientists propose **2 broad views** of the cause of individual prison violence:

    a. The violent individual view

    b. The contextual or structural view

6. **A good theory** of prison violence should also explain violence in other settings.

B. **Legal Rights of Prisoners**

1. The Supreme Court affirmed many constitutional rights of prisoners during the **1960s and after**.

2. During the **1980s and 1990s**, the Court has become **more conservative** in regard to inmate rights.

C. **Managing the Prison**

1. John DiIulio suggests that prison administrators should adopt a **prison-as-mini-government model**.

D. **Prison Reform** is difficult to achieve.

1. The **federal courts** have played a key role in reforming state prison systems.

2. Some observers applaud the increasing **privatization** of prisons as a way to manage prison more efficiently, with less cost.

3. Other observers are concerned about the **potential for problems** and abuses in privately-managed correctional facilities.

E. **Accomplishment of Prison Goals**

1. Prisons **protect the public**, but only while prisoners are behind bars.

2. Many released **inmates are bitter** and ill-prepared to live a law-abiding life.

3. Prison probably has little or **no deterrent effect**.

4. About half of the people in the U.S. see **rehabilitation as an important goal**.

Key Terms

collective behavior/social control model
conflict model (of collective violence)
contextual or structural hypothesis (of individual violence)
correctional treatment
deprivation theory
environment conditions model
importation theory
focal concerns
inmate code
niches
pains of imprisonment
power vacuum model
principle of less eligibility
prison-as-mini-government model
rising expectations/relative deprivation model
spontaneity model
the "nothing works" myth
Title VII

total institution
violent individual hypothesis (of individual violence)

Questions for Study

1. How do deprivation theory and importation theory explain the development of prisoner subcultures?

2. How is the situation of women in prison different from the situation of men?

3. How are prison treatment programs influenced by the principle of less eligibility and the "nothing works" myth?

4. What are some of the duties of correctional officers? What are some difficulties they encounter on the job?

5. What types of prison violence exist? What are some explanations for the causes of prison violence?

6. What legal rights do prisoners have?

7. What is the "prison as mini-government" model of effective prison management?

8. What are some goals of imprisonment? Do you think that the prison accomplishes these goals?

9. In general, how is the prison social environment viewed from the points of view of consensus theory and conflict theory?

Selected Readings

Braswell, Michael, Reid H. Montgomery, Jr., and Lucien X. Lombardo. Prison Violence in America, 2nd ed. (Cincinnati: Anderson, 1994). A collection of readings on the nature and causes of prison violence.

Earley, Pete. The Hot House: Life Inside Leavenworth Prison (New York: Bantam, 1992). After spending a year studying Leavenworth, journalist Earley writes about the violent world inside the walls.

Lombardo, Lucien X. Guards Imprisoned: Correctional Officers at Work, second edition (Cincinnati: Anderson, 1989). Lombardo examines officers' attitudes, how they perform their jobs, and the risks and rewards of prison work as an occupation.

Palmer, Ted. The Re-Emergence of Correctional Intervention (Newbury Park, CA: Sage, 1992). A review of the literature on inmate rehabilitation programs, in which the author concludes that some programs can and do succeed.

Silberman, Matthew. A World of Violence: Corrections in America (Belmont, CA: Wadsworth, 1995). A comprehensive examination of the social, legal, and institutional influences on prison violence.

Toch, Hans. Living in Prison: The Ecology of Survival, revised edition (Hyattsville, MD: American Psychological Association, 1992). A survey of prisoners in maximum security, which highlights the stresses of imprisonment and the ways in which inmates cope.

Zimmer, Lynn E. Women Guarding Men (Chicago: University of Chicago Press, 1986). Details the emergence of women as correctional officers, with emphasis on those who work in maximum security prisons for men.

Sample Test Questions

Multiple Choice Questions

1. Functional subsettings in the prison which contain desired objects, space, resources, people, and relationships between people are referred to by Hans Toch as _____.
    a. hideaways
    b. niches
    c. retreats
    d. dachas

2. An organization in which there is a breakdown of barriers between the basic human activities of sleep, play , and work, and where the staff attempts to control inmates to a strict degree, is known as _____.
    a. a total institution
    b. an asylum
    c. a rest home
    d. a control facility

3. The view that the most important factor in causing prison riots is some unplanned event that sets the collective violence in motion is _____.
    a. the violent individual hypothesis
    b. the deprivation theory
    c. the collective behavior/social control model
    d. the spontaneity model

4.   The deprivation theory of prisonization suggests that the inmate code is a response to _____.
    a.   the influence of gangs outside the prison
    b.   early upbringing of prisoners
    c.   harsh prison conditions
    d.   media portrayals of prisoners

5.   The belief that prisoners should be subject to living conditions that are no better than those experienced by the poorest law-abiding citizens is _____.
    a.   the retribution principle
    b.   the principle of less eligibility
    c.   the restitution principle
    d.   the principle of relative deprivation

6.   Who commits violent acts against whom in prison?
    a.   prisoners commit violence against prisoners
    b.   prisoners commit violence against officers
    c.   officers commit violence against prisoners
    d.   (all of the above)

7.   Which of the following reasons is cited by both men and women as the primary reason they chose to become a correctional officer?
    a.   a chance to control convicted criminals
    b.   the opportunity to wear a uniform
    c.   the pay and benefits
    d.   to gain respect from friends and family

8.   The Supreme court ruled in _____ that prisoners are entitled to legal protection under the Civil Rights Act of 1871, title 42, section 1983.
    a.   *Cooper v. Pate*
    b.   *Johnson v. Avery*
    c.   *Bounds v. Smith*
    d.   *Wolf v. Mcdonnell*

9.   Federal court rulings under the _____ Amendment have limited censorship of prisoner mail, protected the exercise of religious ritual, and provided for access to clergy of many faiths.
    a.   1st
    b.   4th
    c.   5th
    d.   8th

10. Who carries out court-ordered executions?
    a. special citizen executioners
    b. trained hangmen
    c. prison staff
    d. trustee inmates

True/False Questions

T F 11. The norms of the inmate subculture are referred to as the inmate code.

T F 12. Approximately 46 percent of state prisoners are serving time for a violent offense (1996 data).

T F 13. About 15 percent of female inmates are mothers.

T F 14. Most jurisdictions require that correctional officer applicants have completed a 4-year college degree.

T F 15. From a consensus point of view, violence by inmates can be functional.

Essay Questions

16. Who is in prison? That is, what are the social status characteristics (sex, age, race, and other statuses) of imprisoned Americans?

17. Compare and contrast the deprivation model and the importation model of inmate subcultures.

18. What effects do the myth of less eligibility and the "nothing works" myth have on prison treatment programs?

19. What types of violence exist in the prison environment? What are some theories that have been proposed in order to explain the causes of prison violence?

20. Discuss the role that correctional officers play in the prison. Who becomes a correctional officer? What tasks do officers perform? What are some of the rewards and difficulties of the job?

Answers to Sample Test Questions

1b, 2a, 3d, 4c, 5b, 6d, 7c, 8a, 9a, 10c, 11T, 12T, 13F, 14F, 15T

CHAPTER TWELVE
COMMUNITY CORRECTIONS: PROBATION, INTERMEDIATE SANCTIONS, AND PAROLE

Learning Objectives

After completing this chapter, you should understand the following topics:

1. The rationale behind community corrections.

2. The nature of probation programs.

3. How probation and parole programs have been influenced by historical developments in England and America.

4. The responsibilities of probation officers and parole officers.

5. The various types of intermediate sanctions, and what each is intended to accomplish.

6. Why parole is declining in influence at the same time intermediate sanctions and probation are increasing in scope.

7. The issues of "widening the net" and recidivism.

8. How our thinking about community corrections programs may be guided by the consensus and conflict theoretical perspectives.

Chapter Summary

1. Community corrections consists of criminal sanctions that take place outside of the jail or prison setting. They include probation, intermediate sanctions, and parole.

2. Probation allows offenders to remain in the community under the supervision of a probation officer, subject to conditions. There are more persons on probation in the United States than there are under any other form of correctional supervision.

3. Intermediate sanctions are intended to be harsher than probation but less harsh than imprisonment. Typical intermediate sanctions include fines, restitution, community service, intensive supervision probation, electronic monitoring, shock incarceration, and asset forfeiture.

4.   Parole allows the release of prison inmates from incarceration into the community, where they are supervised by a parole officer.

5.   Community corrections also encompasses programs intended to ease released prisoners' transition from the institution to the community. These include work release programs, furloughs, and halfway houses.

6.   From a conflict point of view, critics charge that community corrections programs may result in widening the net, when persons who would not otherwise have gone to prison are sentenced to community corrections programs. This has the result of increasing the amount of social control exerted by the criminal justice process.

7.   Another key concern about community corrections is recidivism, the involvement of ex-offenders in new crimes. Studies show that nearly half of all prison inmates have served time for previous convictions.

8.   The future appears bright for intermediate sanctions, which seem to offer benefits for both liberals and conservatives. Parole appears to be on the decline, while probation remains the largest component of American corrections.

9.   Consensus and conflict theories suggest questions that we can ask in order to deepen our understanding of community corrections. The most fundamental question concerns whether these programs benefit society as a whole, or whether benefits are felt primarily by government and powerful groups.

Chapter Outline

Introduction

A.   Prison may be **the best sentence** for some offenders.

B.   But for some offenders, **community corrections** may be the best option.

C.   **Community corrections** consists of criminal sanctions that do not take place in the traditional prison or jail setting. It includes:

    1.   **Probation**

    2.   **Intermediate Sanctions**

    3.   **Parole**

I. **_Probation_** (def): A program in which final action on offenders' cases is suspended so that they remain at liberty, subject to conditions imposed by a court, under the supervision and guidance of a probation worker.

    A. **History of Probation -**

        1.   1841 and after: **John Augustus** paid bail of convicted offenders in Boston court. They were turned over to him for supervision.

        2.   **By 1930**, 36 states and the federal government had probation laws in force.

        3.   Probation officers in the 19th century were often **ill-trained** and subject to **political influences**. In the 20th century, probation has been beset by **high case loads**.

        4.   **Consensus theory** - probation allows offenders to be rehabilitated while remaining in the community, and everyone benefits.

        5.   **Conflict theory** - Probation makes the job of judges and attorneys easier, but does not necessarily benefit others.

    B. **Structure of Probation -**

        1.   More than 2,000 probation agencies **at federal, state, and local levels**.

        2.   **More people are on probation** than any other type of correctional supervision, including prison, jail, and parole.

        3.   About **58 percent** of persons under correctional supervision are on probation (1995 data).

        4.   About **2/3 of persons** convicted of felonies and misdemeanors are sentenced to probation.

    C. **Administration of Probation -**

        1.   **Probation begins** after a person has been found guilty at trial, or has pleaded guilty.

        2.   Probationers must observe certain **conditions** or their probation may be **revoked** and they must go to jail or prison.

3. **Probation officers** have two primary responsibilities:

    a.   Preparing **presentence investigation reports (PSI reports)**.

    b.   **Supervising offenders** who are on probation.

4. **Consensus theory** - Probation benefits society by keeping certain offenders out of jail or prison.

5. **Conflict theory** - Probation may simply be a way for the government to exert social control over more of its people.

6. **"A Day in the Life of a Federal Probation Officer" - Criminal Justice in Action** box on page 368 illustrates the probation officer's law enforcement and treatment responsibilities.

II. *Intermediate Sanctions* - So-called because they lie between the harshness of a prison sentence and the relative leniency of probation. Typical intermediate sanctions are listed below:

A. **Fines and Restitution** -

    1.   **Fine** - An amount of money that is paid to the court.

    2.   **Restitution** - Compensation paid to the victim.

B. **Community Service** - Allows offenders to pay back society by working in the community.

C. **Intensive supervision probation (ISP)** - Typically involve closer supervision, unannounced drug testing, strict enforcement of conditions, and required participation in programs of treatment, employment, or community service.

    1.   Research suggests that ISP has **little effect on recidivism**, and it is expensive.

D. **Electronic Monitoring** - Sometimes referred to as "house arrest."

E. **Shock Incarceration** - "Boot camps."

    1.   **By 1996**, the federal government and more than 32 states were operating boot camp programs.

2.   **Programs involve** military-style discipline, physical activity, and intensive treatment programming.

3.   Research suggests that shock incarceration may not reduce **recidivism**. Still, it **remains popular** among politicians, the public, and many alumni of the programs.

F.   **Asset Forfeiture** - Loss of rights to personal property as a result of suspected involvement in criminal activity.

1.   **Civil Forfeiture** - An action against property.

2.   **Criminal Forfeiture** - Authorized by the Racketeer-Influenced and Corrupt Organizations Act (RICO) in 1970.

3.   Civil forfeiture activities have brought a **great deal of money** to law enforcement agencies, who share the proceeds of sale of forfeited items.

4.   Some **observers are concerned** that forfeiture violates citizens' constitutional rights.

III.   *Parole* - (def.) A program in which convicted offenders, after serving a portion of their sentence in prison or jail, are conditionally released in the community under the supervision of a parole worker.

Parole include **3 fundamental elements**:

1.   Discretionary **early release** from prison.

2.   **Supervision** of prisoners who have been released into the community.

3.   **Revocation** of parole status if conditions of release are violated.

To **remember the difference** between probation and parole: probation occurs "before" prison, while parole occurs "after."

A.   **History of Parole** -

1.   British practice, beginning in 1597, of **transportation** of convicts to faraway colonies.

2.   **Ticket of leave** granted to certain British prisoners after 1853.

3. **Captain Alexander Maconochie** (1787-1860) instituted program of **marks** at Norfolk Island prison, near Australia.

4. **Sir Walter Crofton** (1815-1897) was named Director of Irish prison system in 1854. His **Irish mark system** combined a prison sentence with a ticket of leave.

5. In America, the chief architect of the **reformatory era** after 1870 was **Zebulon Brockway**, warden of Elmira Reformatory. Certain prisoners were released into the community before completing their sentence, on good behavior.

6. 1850s and 1860s - **Michigan** granted its governor the power to release prisoners under conditional pardons.

7. **By 1930**, all states and the federal government had parole programs.

B. **Structure of Parole -**

1. Administered at the state level by a **state parole board**, which holds **parole hearings**.

2. Parolees are released to the community, under the **supervision** of a parole officer.

3. According to Irwin and Austin, about 60 percent of parolees **return to prison**.

    a. **Consensus theory** - High rate of parole failure may mean that parole is working well by holding parolees to the highest standards.

    b. **Conflict theory** - High rate of parole failure may mean that ex-offenders--one of society's most powerless groups--is being subjected to unwarranted governmental control.

4. The job of **parole officer** is often a difficult one, with high caseloads, few resources, and little public support.

C. **The Attack on Parole**

1. Beginning in the 1970s, parole was **increasingly criticized**.

2.　According to Keith Bottomley, attacks on parole and indeterminate sentencing **followed four arguments**:

    a.　Some argued that parole is **ineffective in reducing recidivism**.

    b.　Some argued that parole and the indeterminate sentence **place too much power** in the hands of government.

    c.　Some argued that there are **no standard criteria** for awarding or denying parole release.

    d.　Finally, liberals and conservatives joined to embrace the new **justice model**, which advocates less rehabilitation and harsher punishment.

3.　In 1987, the **federal government abolished parole** for federal prisoners, and instituted a system of **sentencing guidelines**.

D.　**Pre-Release Programs**

1.　**Work release** - Inmates allowed to work in the community and return to prison at night.

2.　**Furloughs** - Short period of unsupervised release from prison.

3.　**Halfway Houses** - Intended to be a home-like setting in the community. Halfway between the prison and the community.

IV.　*Issues in Community Corrections*

A.　**Widening the Net** - Do community corrections programs bring more people into the net of government control?

1.　People's position on net-widening depends on their **ideological point of view**.

B.　**Recidivism** - Public policy must balance the risk of releasing offenders into the community against the costs of imprisoning them.

C.　**The Future of Community Corrections -**

1.　Community corrections programs will probably **continue to increase** in number and scope.

2.   The **consensus perspective** leads us to ask if community corrections programs benefit society by assisting offenders.

3.   The **conflict approach** leads us to ask if community corrections programs benefit government and the powerful by subjecting more and more people to criminal justice control.

Key Terms

community corrections
community service
day fines
electronic monitoring
fixed fine system
furlough
halfway house
intensive supervision probation (ISP)
intermediate sanctions
parole
presentence investigation (PSI)
probation
recidivism
restitution
shock incarceration (boot camp)
widening the net
work release

Questions for Study

1.   What is the rationale for community corrections? In other words, what are the various community corrections programs intended to accomplish?

2.   What was the contribution of John Augustus to the history of probation?

3.   What is the meaning of the term "intermediate sanctions?"

4.   List some typical intermediate sanctions, and describe each of them.

5.   Discuss highlights of the history of parole. What important ideas were advanced by Alexander Maconochie, Walter Crofton, and Zebulon Brockway?

6.   On what grounds did the practice of parole come under attack during the 1970s?

7.   Do you think that community corrections programs "widen the net?" Why or why not?

8.   Why is recidivism a threat to community corrections programs? What, if anything, do you think can be done to reduce recidivism?

9.   What benefits do you think community corrections provide to the offenders involved, to the wider community, to government, and to society's powerful interest groups?

Selected Readings

John Augustus, John Augustus: First Probation Officer (Montclair, NJ: Patterson Smith, 1972. Originally published 1852). A short description of his work, by the founder of American probation.

David E. Duffee and Edmund F. McGarrell, eds., Community Corrections: A Community Field Approach (Cincinnati, OH: Anderson, 1990). A theoretically-sophisticated collection of papers relating to influences of the wider community on community corrections, and vice-versa.

Doris Layton MacKenzie and Eugene E. Hebert, eds., Correctional Boot Camps: A Tough Intermediate Sanction, Research Report (Washington, DC: U.S. Department of Justice, National Institute of Justice, 1995). A collection of articles on boot camp-related research sponsored by the National Institute of Justice.

Norval Morris and Michael Tonry, Between Prison and Probation: Intermediate Punishments in a Rational Sentencing System (New York: Oxford University Press, 1990). A comprehensive and theoretically-informed review of intermediate punishments.

Uglješa Zvekić, ed., Alternatives to Imprisonment in Comparative Perspective, (Chicago: Nelson-Hall, 1994). Examines alternatives to incarceration in Africa, the Arab Countries, Asia, Australia, Europe, North America, Latin America, and the Caribbean.

Sample Test Questions

Multiple Choice Questions

1.   _____ is when a former inmate returns to prison for another offense.
    a.   restitution
    b.   retribution
    c.   recidivism
    d.   reductionism

2. _____ are criminal sentences that are not as severe or confining as incarceration, but which are more severe and confining than probation.
   a.   Capital punishments
   b.   Community corrections programs
   c.   Intermediate sanctions
   d.   Intermediate guidelines

3. _____ is the fear that alternative punishments may not provide an alternative to imprisonment because they might simply capture a new population of offenders.
   a.   Widening the net
   b.   Opening the doors
   c.   Casting the lure
   d.   Hunting the fox

4. A _____ is a short period of unsupervised release from prison, granted for a specific purpose such as a death in the immediate family.
   a.   halfway house
   b.   pardon
   c.   work release
   d.   furlough

5. A program that allows prison inmates to be released into the community before the expiration of their sentence is _____.
   a.   probation
   b.   intermediate sanctions
   c.   parole
   d.   incarceration

6. Shock incarceration programs usually include which of the following components?
   a.   military-style discipline
   b.   physical exercise
   c.   intensive treatment programming
   d.   (all of the above)

7. Which of the following is generally recognized as a forerunner of modern parole?
   a.   the British practice of transportation
   b.   ticket of leave
   c.   the Irish mark system
   d.   (all of the above)

8.   In _____, Congress abolished parole for persons convicted of federal crimes.
       a.   1935
       b.   1967
       c.   1987
       d.   1995

9.   All persons who are under probation or parole supervision must _____.
       a.   abide by certain conditions
       b.   return to prison each day
       c.   perform community service
       d.   take classes to receive their diploma or GED

10.   _____ involve(s) money that is paid to the offender.
       a.   Restitution
       b.   Retribution
       c.   Fines
       d.   Crime taxes

True/False Questions

T F 11.   Shock incarceration facilities are also popularly known as boot camps.

T F 12.   Presentence investigation reports (PSI reports) are prepared by parole officers.

T F 13.   According to consensus theory, probation benefits society by keeping certain offenders out of prison or jail.

T F 14.   According to the author of the text, the use of parole will probably continue to decline in the first decades of the coming century.

T F 15.   One of the primary criticisms of parole is that the criteria used to grant or deny parole release are vague and unreliable.

Essay Questions

16.   What is community corrections, and what are community corrections programs designed to accomplish?

17.   Compare and contrast probation programs with parole release programs. How are they similar? How are they different?

18.   Discuss community corrections programs from the perspectives of consensus theory and conflict theory.

19.   What are intermediate sanctions? Do they accomplish what they are designed to accomplish?

20.   Discuss the "Day in the Life of a Federal Probation Officer" box on page 368 of the text. What does this vignette illustrate about the job of probation officer?

Answers to Sample Test Questions

1c, 2c, 3a, 4d, 5c, 6d, 7d, 8c, 9a, 10a, 11T, 12F, 13T, 14T, 15T

CHAPTER THIRTEEN
JUVENILE JUSTICE

Learning Objectives

After completing this chapter, you should understand the following topics:

1. The nature and extent of juvenile crime and status offenses.

2. How wayward children have been treated from the colonial era to the present day.

3. The importance of houses of refuge and the juvenile court.

4. How the juvenile court differs from adult criminal court.

5. Typical stages of juvenile justice processing.

6. Current controversies in juvenile justice, including juveniles accused of federal offenses, disparate processing by sex and race, and capital punishment.

7. How the consensus and conflict theoretical perspectives help us understand the dominant theme in American juvenile justice, which is the tension between controlling wayward young people versus helping them.

Chapter Summary

1. During the colonial era, children who misbehaved were most often dealt with by their families. As American society developed, control of juvenile offenders became a function of the state.

2. Nineteenth-Century efforts to manage juvenile offenders centered around Houses of Refuge (reformatories). The state justified its intervention in the parent/child relationship by invoking the legal doctrine of *parens patriae*.

3. Juvenile courts were designed to remove young offenders from the adult criminal court and to provide them with an informal and nonadversarial setting in which to have their cases resolved. However, juveniles lacked the protection of constitutional rights, and juvenile court proceedings often failed to protect the children's best interests.

4. Although the majority of juvenile justice processing occurs at the state level, the federal government has played a major role in shaping the direction of the nation's juvenile justice policy. For instance, the Juvenile Justice and Delinquency

Prevention Act of 1974 mandated sweeping changes, such as the removal of status offenders from secure facilities.

5. The juvenile justice process has frequently punished female offenders for failure to conform to society's traditional gender roles.

6. Stages of the juvenile justice process include arrest, intake, adjudication, disposition, and aftercare.

7. Concerns about American juvenile justice include differential treatment by race and sex, transfer of juveniles to adult criminal court, and capital punishment for persons who commit crimes while juveniles. As the new century dawns, some scholars believe that the system should be abolished, while others seek ways to improve current methods.

Chapter Outline

(Part 5 Opener) The Case of Willie Bosket illustrates the fundamental dilemma of juvenile justice: how to treat juveniles as the children they are while protecting society from juvenile crime.

Introduction

A. Persons under the age of 18 are referred to as **juveniles** under the law.

B. Criminal acts by juveniles are known as **delinquency**.

C. **Status offenses** are behaviors that are prohibited for juveniles but not for adults.

I. *Juvenile Crime and Status Offenses*

A. Juveniles are involved in about **1/4 of all violent crimes**.

B. Arrests of juveniles for violent crimes are expected to **double by 2010**.

C. the U.S. Department of Justice reports that juvenile **homicide arrests tripled** between 1984 and 1994, and that the increase was related to **easy availability of firearms**

D. Juvenile crime is also a problem in the nation's **schools**.

E. **Youth gangs** are found in all 50 states.

F.　　Use of **illegal drugs** by juveniles is a particular concern.

II.　*History of Juvenile Justice*

A.　**The Colonial Era -**

1.　**Children under age 7** are considered incapable of criminal responsibility. This is an ancient distinction borrowed from English Common Law.

2.　**Children between 7 and 14** are considered incapable of criminal intent in most cases.

3.　The **Stubborn Child Statute (1646)** was the first American law providing punishments for juveniles. Enacted by General Court of Massachusetts Bay Colony. This law **foreshadowed later components** of American juvenile policy:

a.　Required children to conform to a standard different from adults.

b.　Codified childrens' obligation to obey their parents.

c.　Affirmed government right to intervene in parent/child relationship.

B.　**Reformatories (Houses of Refuge) -**

1.　The first juvenile reformatory was the **New York House of Refuge**, opened in New York City in 1825.

2.　Later, Boston's **House of Reformation** (1826) and Philadelphia's **House of Refuge** (1828).

3.　Houses of refuge recognized **3 classes of wayward children**: criminal offenders, status offenders, and cases of parental neglect.

4.　Conditions at the houses of refuge were dismal.

5.　Many children were **placed out**: sent on trains to live and work far away.

6.　Ideology of the juvenile reformatory embodied in the legal doctrine of *parens patriae*, which is the idea that the state has an overwhelming interest in protecting the welfare of children, and that this interest supersedes the interests of parents.

7.   The case of *Ex parte Crouse* incorporated the *parens patriae* doctrine into American law.

8.   In the second half of the 19th century, the **Child Savers** criticized the reformatories and advocated family-type environments.

9.   Between 1900 and 1950, the juvenile reformatory grew and expanded. It later turned into the **juvenile correctional facility**, with less emphasis on rehabilitation and higher levels of violence.

C.   **The Juvenile Court** -

1.   The **first juvenile court** in America was established in Chicago, Illinois in 1899. By 1917, all but three states had established juvenile courts.

2.   Juvenile courts were **different from adult courts**:

     a.   **Treatment-based ideology** rather than punitive ideology.

     b.   **Hearings held in private** rather than in view of the public.

     c.   **Informal** nature of juvenile court proceedings.

     d.   Proceedings intended to be **nonadversarial** and benevolent.

3.   Despite good intentions, juveniles had **few rights** in juvenile court.

D.   **The Juvenile Rights Era** -

1.   For most of the history of the U.S., juveniles did not hold the same rights as adults. **Few legal protections**, and often harsh punishments.

2.   *In re Gault* (1967) radically altered American juvenile justice by reaffirming that juveniles facing institutional commitment possess many constitutional rights:

     a.   Right to counsel, and right to have counsel appointed if they cannot afford one,

     b.   Right to be notified of the petition (charges),

     c.   Right to be given timely notice of hearings,

        d.   Right to remain silent and refuse to testify at hearings,

        e.   Right to confront witnesses and cross-examine them through their attorneys.

3.   The President's Commission on Law Enforcement and Administration of Justice (1967) produced their influential report entitled <u>The Challenge of Crime in a Free Society</u>. The report called for:

        a.   decriminalization of juvenile status offenses,

        b.   diversion of juveniles from juvenile courts to treatment programs,

        c.   granting juveniles the same due process rights enjoyed by adults in criminal court,

        d.   a focus on deinstitutionalization,

        e.   decentralization and diversification of juvenile services.

4.   The **Juvenile Justice and Delinquency Prevention Act of 1974** has been very influential.

        a.   Required states to stop placing status offenders in secure facilities,

        b.   and to separate juveniles and adults in confinement.

        c.   Required that 75 percent of funds received by the states was to be used for community-based programming.

E.   **Criminalization of Juvenile Justice**

1.   After the *Gault* decision, the juvenile court has lost much of its distinctiveness.

2.   Juvenile courts now much more closely **resemble adult criminal courts**.

3.   This change was aided by **citizens' fear** of juvenile crime, the **conservative shift** in the 1980s and 1990s, and government **get-tough-on-crime** initiatives.

4. More juveniles are being **transferred to criminal court (waiver of jurisdiction)**, and adjudicated as adults. Most have been accused of violent crimes.

III. *The Juvenile Justice Process*

A. **Arrest** -

B. **Intake** -

1. Cases that are referred to juvenile court are **screened by an intake officer**, usually a juvenile probation officer, who has a great deal of discretion as to how to handle each case.

2. If sufficient evidence exists to continue prosecution, then a **petition is filed**, which specifies the charges to be adjudicated in juvenile court.

3. At a **detention hearing**, the judge decides whether the juvenile should be held, transferred to adult court, or released.

C. **Adjudication** -

1. Juveniles appear in juvenile court at an **adjudicatory hearing**, which is like a trial in adult court.

D. **Disposition** -

1. A **disposition** is like a sentence in adult court.

2. **Juvenile dispositions include** fines, probation, drug or alcohol treatment, foster care, victim restitution, community service, confinement in a juvenile detention facility, confinement in a residential facility, or a combination of these.

3. **Correctional facilities for juveniles** vary along 3 dimensions:

a. Long-term facilities versus short-term facilities

b. Institutional facilities versus open facilities

c. Public facilities versus private facilities

4. Correctional facilities for juveniles form a **separate prison system** in the United States.

E. **Aftercare -**

1. **Similar to parole** for adult offenders.

2. Juveniles participate in aftercare programs **after they have been released** from a juvenile institution.

IV. *Issues in Juvenile Justice*

A. **Juveniles Accused of Federal Offenses -**

1. There is **no federal juvenile justice system**.

2. Most juveniles accused of federal offenses are **referred to state authorities**.

3. The U.S. Attorney General can choose to **retain jurisdiction** over a juvenile accused of a federal offense.

B. **Disparate Processing by Race and Sex -**

1. Black juveniles are processed as **status offenders** at a rate 1/3 higher than whites.

2. Black juveniles are **over represented at all stages** of the juvenile justice process.

3. **Research** has not yet established why this disparity by race exists.

4. **Female juveniles** make up about 42 percent of status offense cases but only 15 percent of delinquency cases. Girls are placed in juvenile custody for offenses that are less serious than the offenses that get boys detained or committed.

5. Disparate treatment of blacks and females illustrates **a prediction of the conflict perspective**, that relatively powerless groups will be dominated by more powerful groups.

C.   **Juveniles and The Death Penalty -**

      1.   The **first recorded execution** of a juvenile took place in 1642.

      2.   In *Stanford v. Kentucky* (1989), the Supreme Court ruled that execution of a juvenile who is 15 years old or less is unconstitutional.

D.   **Juvenile Justice in the New Century -**

      1.   Carl Pope suggests that **3 issues must be resolved** regarding juvenile justice in the 21st century:

            a.   Whether juvenile justice should be abolished or kept,

            b.   What changes should be made in juvenile justice processing, and

            c.   Which juveniles should come before the juvenile court.

Key Terms

adjudicatory hearing
aftercare
Child Savers
delinquency
detention hearing
Houses of Refuge
institutional and open facilities
intake
Juvenile Justice and Delinquency Prevention Act
juvenile probation officer
nonoffenders
parens patriae
reformatories
status offenses
Stubborn Child Statute
transfer (to criminal court)
waiver petition

Questions for Study

      1.   How have misbehaving children been dealt with in the colonial era, the 19th century, and in recent decades?

2. How might the rise of houses of refuge be interpreted by the consensus and conflict perspectives?

3. What was the juvenile court set up to accomplish? How did it improve the lot of delinquents and status offenders? What negative outcomes did it produce?

4. In what ways have female delinquents and status offenders been treated differently than their male counterparts?

5. Describe the typical sequence of stages that make up the juvenile justice process.

6. Why are some juvenile offenders sent to adult criminal court instead of being processed in juvenile court? Do you believe that this is a good thing? Why or why not?

7. What changes do you feel need to be made in American juvenile justice in the 21st century? Are your ideas closest to the consensus or conflict perspective?

Selected Readings

Thomas J. Bernard, The Cycle of Juvenile Justice (New York: Oxford University Press, 1992). A social history of American juvenile justice.

Fox Butterfield, All God's Children: The Bosket Family and the American Tradition of Violence (New York: Alfred A. Knopf). As a young teenager, Willie Bosket was found guilty of two murders committed in the New York City subway. His case led the New York State legislature to pass a law lowering the age at which juveniles could be processed as adults.

Dean J. Champion and G. Larry Mays, Transferring Juveniles to Criminal Courts: Trends and Implications for Criminal Justice (New York: Praeger, 1991). As a result of "get-tough" policies, more and more juveniles are being waived to criminal court. Champion and Mays examine the results of this trend.

Meda Chesney-Lind and Randall G. Shelden, Girls, Delinquency, and Juvenile Justice, (Pacific Grove, CA: Brooks/Cole, 1992). An analysis of the social definition of female delinquency as a product of the control of female sexuality in patriarchal society.

Charles Patrick Ewing, Kids Who Kill, (Lexington, MA: Lexington, 1990). A fascinating and frightening study of juveniles who commit homicide.

Office of Juvenile Justice and Delinquency Prevention, Juvenile Offenders and Victims: a National Report, (Washington, D.C.: U.S. Department of Justice, 1995). A detailed and timely report on all aspects of juvenile crime and justice.

Anthony M. Platt, <u>The Child Savers: The Invention of Delinquency</u>, (Chicago: University of Chicago Press, 1969). A perceptive study of American society's creation of the idea of juvenile delinquency, with particular focus on the Child Savers movement and the creation of the juvenile court in Illinois during the late 19th century.

Sample Test Questions

Multiple Choice Questions

1. A juvenile court proceeding in which a judge reviews the evidence and determines whether a young person should be adjudicated delinquent is a(n) _____.
    a. juvenile trial
    b. adjudicatory hearing
    c. detention hearing
    d. bifurcated trial

2. Behaviors that are legally prohibited for juveniles but not for adults are known as _____.
    a. juvenile crimes
    b. juvenile delinquency
    c. status offenses
    d. childhood offenses

3. The first American law to provide punishments for recalcitrant children was _____, enacted by the General Court of Massachusetts Bay Colony in 1646.
    a. the Stubborn Child Statute
    b. the Juvenile Delinquency Act
    c. the Recalcitrant Children Statute
    d. the Boston Delinquency Act

4. _____ is the stage of the juvenile justice process at which specialized juvenile processing begins.
    a. Arrest
    b. Intake
    c. Adjudication
    d. The preliminary hearing

5. A delinquent act in the juvenile system is analogous to a _____ in the adult criminal justice system.
    a. misdemeanor
    b. violation
    c. crime
    d. traffic offense

6.   Juvenile correctional facilities are never referred to as _____.
       a.   training schools
       b.   prisons
       c.   camps
       d.   residential facilities

7.   Which of the following Supreme Court cases marked the beginning of the criminalization of the juvenile court?
       a.   *Schall v. Martin*
       b.   *Eddings v. Oklahoma*
       c.   *Oklahoma Publishing Co. v. District Court*
       d.   *In re Gault*

8.   _____ involves programs that juveniles participate in after they have been released from the custody of a juvenile correctional institution.
       a.   Parole
       b.   Aftercare
       c.   Transfer
       d.   Waiver

9.   According to FBI data, juveniles are responsible for about _____ percent of the murders that occur in the United States.
       a.   10
       b.   20
       c.   40
       d.   50

10.   According to a survey by the National Youth Gang Center, there are youth gangs in _____ U.S. states.
       a.   35
       b.   41
       c.   47
       d.   50

True/False Questions

T F 11.   A disposition in juvenile court is similar to a sentence in adult criminal court.

T F 12.   The Supreme Court has ruled that execution of a person who was age 17 or less at the time of the crime is unconstitutional.

T F 13.   The first juvenile court in America was established in 1901 in San Francisco, California.

T F 14.   The first juvenile reformatory in the United States was the Founder's Institute, established in 1903.

T F 15.   In 1967, the President's Commission on Law Enforcement and Administration of Justice called for, among other things, the decriminalization of juvenile status offenses.

Essay Questions

16.   Discuss the concept of childhood and how it applies to the structure and process of juvenile justice.

17.   From a conflict perspective, the history of juvenile justice is a story of increasing involvement of the state in the affairs of children and their families. Discuss this issue in relation to the house of refuge movement.

18.   Compare and contrast the juvenile court with adult criminal court. How are these two types of courts similar? How are they different? What rights do juveniles have before the juvenile court?

19.   Trace the typical stages of the juvenile justice process, from intake to aftercare.

20.   How has the juvenile justice process treated young women differently than young men?

Answers to Sample Test Questions

1b, 2c, 3a, 4b, 5c, 6b, 7d, 8b, 9a, 10d, 11T, 12F, 13F, 14F, 15T

CHAPTER FOURTEEN
VICTIMS' RIGHTS

Learning Objectives

After completing this chapter, you should understand the following topics:

1.   The meaning of the concept of crime victim.

2.   How the victims' movement arose to become an important advocate for victims' rights.

3.   How the risks of becoming a crime victim vary according to peoples' status characteristics.

4.   Theories of victimization, including lifestyle-exposure theory and routine activities theory.

5.   The rights that victims possess at each stage of the criminal justice process.

6.   Programs that have been developed to aid victims of crime.

7.   Ways that victims and potential victims sometimes act to protect themselves and to retaliate against their victimizers.

Chapter Summary

1.   Crime victims experience harm due to a criminal act. Victims include individuals, groups, and society itself.

2.   The victim's movement has directed attention toward the plight of certain crime victims.

3.   Risks of becoming a crime victim vary according to social status characteristics. The highest rates of victimization in recent years have been experienced by young black males. This group is particularly at risk for firearm-related homicide.

4.   Important theories of victimization include lifestyle-exposure theory and routine activities theory.

5.   Crime victims have been allowed to play an increasingly visible role in criminal proceedings in recent decades. One of the most important activities of victims is presentation of their opinions and feelings to the court in the form of a victim impact statement, or in person through the allocution privilege.

6. Crime victims may seek to recover some of their monetary losses through restitution programs, civil litigation, crime insurance payments, and government-sponsored compensation programs.

7. Some crime victims and their families seek self-help outside of the criminal justice system, in the form of self-protection, retaliation, and other forms of social control from below. Some of these measures are encouraged by criminal justice officials, while others are prohibited by law.

8. The consensus and conflict perspectives help us to understand the situation of crime victims. Consensus theory suggests that crime victims can voice the community's outrage over crime. Conflict theory shows how the interests of victims and criminal justice agencies often differ.

Chapter Outline

Introduction

A. The **primary goal of criminal justice** is prosecuting offenders, not satisfying victims.

B. According to law, **crimes are offenses against the state**, not against the individuals or groups who are harmed.

C. However, in recent years criminal justice agencies have **worked to include victims** whenever possible.

D. For some, the harm from their victimization is **permanent**.

I.   Victims of Crime

Crime victims are persons or groups who experience harm as the result of a criminal act.

Victimology is the scientific study of victims.

The direct monetary costs of crime add up to a **"yearly crime tax"** of $425 for each U.S. citizen.

A.   **The Victims' Movement** -

1. As crime victims developed an **awareness of their common plight**, the victims' movement was born. (victims as an interest group illustrates conflict theory)

2. **Several factors** in the late 1960s and early 1970s led to victims movement:

    a. **Crime rates** rose.

    b. Media accounts fueled public **fear of crime**.

    c. **Politicians** seized on the issue of law and order, and increased funds for crime control.

    d. The **civil rights movement** provided a model.

    e. The **courts** issued many rulings supporting the rights of criminal suspects and prison inmates.

    f. The **feminist movement** sensitized the public to crimes against women.

3. In the 1970s, the Law Enforcement Assistance Administration (of the U.S. Department of Justice) funded creation of **victim/witness assistance centers** in local prosecutor's offices.

4. **Victims' organizations** were created, such as Mothers Against Drunk Driving (MADD), and Parents of Murdered Children.

5. Robert Elias suggests that politicians may have manipulated the victims' movement to increase support for law-and-order **political agendas.**

    a. Elias notes that current definition of victim focuses on individual victims and **excludes entire classes of victims** such as neglected children and persons harmed by government repression.

    b. Elias further notes that current victim policy **ignores structural victimization** that is caused by the way society is organized.

    c. Elias points out that current victim policy **embraces the conservative agenda** while excluding liberal political agendas such as rehabilitation and suspect's due process rights. For example, the **War on Drugs**.

6. **International human rights efforts** can be viewed as a type of international victim's movement.

B.   **Characteristics of Crime Victims** - (see Figure 14.1 on page 430)

    1.   Victimization data are gathered through the **National Crime Victimization Survey (NCVS),** administered since 1972 by the U.S. Department of Justice.

    2.   **Black male teens** have the highest violent victimization rates.

    3.   **Elderly white females** have the lowest risk.

    4.   Juveniles between 12-19 made up **1/3 of all violent crime victims** in 1996. This is the highest rate for all age groups.

    5.   **Rates of homicide** increased sharply for younger age groups since the mid-1980s. Black juveniles aged 14-17 were 5 times more likely than whites to become victims of homicide during the years 1976-1991.

    6.   Many victimizations involve **firearms**.

    7.   Rates of victimization appear to be **on the decline since 1994.**

C.   **Theories of Victimization** -

    1.   **Victim-precipitated crime** involves situations where the actions of persons lead directly to their becoming crime victims.

    2.   We must be careful to avoid the fallacy of **blaming the victim.** Crime victims are not responsible for their victimization.

    3.   **Victimization theories** look at the behavior of victims and potential victims (see Figure 14.4 and Figure 14.5 on page 434):

        a.   **Lifestyle-Exposure Theory** (Hindelang, Gottfredson, and Garofalo): Persons whose lifestyle patterns bring them into contact with high-risk persons, in high-risk places, at particularly dangerous times of day are more likely to become victims.

        b.   **Routine Activities Theory** (Cohen and Felson): Risks of victimization increase when there is a motivated offender, a suitable target, and an absence of capable guardians to prevent the victimization.

        1.   Recent research has focused on **"hot spots"** of crime, such as areas near bars and taverns.

II. *The Rights of Victims* -

The role of victims has been expanding at each stage of the criminal justice process. The criminal justice process may benefit all of society, including victims (**consensus theory**). However, the interests of victims often differ from those of criminal justice agencies and officials (**conflict theory**).

A. Before and During Trial -

1. Victims are expected to **report the crime** and to **cooperate with police** and prosecutors.

B. At Plea Bargaining and Sentencing

1. This stage is particularly **important to victims,** because it sets the punishment for the convicted offender.

2. The federal government and all 50 states have enacted **victim participation legislation** that permits victims to express their views of appropriate sentences.

    a. A **victim impact statement** is a written statement by the victim, which is sometimes included in the reports prepared by probation officers.

    b. **Allocution** is the expression of views by victims in a face-to-face, verbal appearance in court.

3. Some scholars have criticized victim participation legislation on the grounds that it is **not fair** for victims to influence sentencing, which should be based solely on the facts of the case.

4. Victim participation may make **victims feel better,** but research has failed to show that it has **any measurable effect** on sentencing.

C. In Probation and Parole Decisions -

1. **Probation** is granted at the sentencing phase, where victims may submit a victim impact statement or address the court directly (allocution).

2. By 1996, 43 states had passed legislation allowing victims to **attend parole hearings** to express their opinions about the offender's early release.

3. Research suggests that the presence of a victim impact statement **may have a strong effect** on parole boards' decision to grant or deny parole release.

III. *Programs for Crime Victims* -

A. **Restitution by the Offender** involves payment of a dollar amount to the victim(s).

1. Most sentences **do not include restitution**, and many offenders who are ordered to pay restitution **do not comply**.

2. According to Andrew Karmen, restitution is a **"leaky net"** that lets many offenders through its holes.

B. **Civil Litigation**, also known as **tort claims**.

1. Most people who have been harmed **do not file a civil claim**.

C. **Insurance Repayments** -

1. Some victims receive compensation through **private homeowner's or business insurance.**

2. In 1970 the federal government created the **Federal Crime Insurance Fund** to insure businesses and individuals who are unable to obtain private crime insurance.

D. **Government Compensation Programs** -

1. Congress passed the **Victims of Crime Act (VOCA)** in 1984, which creates a **Crime Victims Fund** to provide states with victim compensation funds.

2. **Most states** now offer some form of victim compensation, but eligibility and level of funding varies from state to state.

E. **Limiting Criminals' Profits** -

1. Laws that limit criminals profits are **very popular** with the public, but they have encountered **legal difficulty**.

2. In 1977, New York state passed the "**Son of Sam**" law allowing the state to confiscate profits earned by criminals from their crime.

3. The **Federal Victim and Witness Protection Act of 1982** requires publishers to pay a victims fund any compensation from a criminal's story.

4. In *Simon and Schuster v. Members of the New York State Crime Victims Board* (1991), the Supreme Court struck down laws limiting criminals' profits on the grounds that they violate the right to free speech.

IV. *Victim Self-Help* is where victims or potential victims act on their own to protect themselves, to defend themselves, or to punish their victimizers.

A. **Protective Measures**: buying a gun, carrying tear gas, attending self-defense classes, installing burglar alarms, and other activities.

B. **Resistance** - Actively resisting or killing an intruder or attacker.

1. **Verbal** resistance -

2. **Physical** resistance -

3. **Armed** resistance -

4. Research suggests that **resistance may be effective**.

C. **Retaliation and Vigilantism** -

1. Under the law, victims cannot **take the law into their own hands**. They must let the criminal justice process do its work.

2. Nevertheless, some victims engage in **retaliation and vigilantism**.

3. **Social control from below** (Baumgartner) refers to situations where persons with lesser power punish persons with greater power. This has some relevance to the situation of victims and offenders.

a. **Rebellion** - open violence.

b. **Covert retaliation** - secret revenge.

c.   **Noncooperation** - refusing to do something that is expected.

d.   **Appeals for support** - enlisting the assistance of a powerful ally.

e.   **Flight** - removing oneself from the situation.

f.   **Distress** - engaging in behavior that shows one is incapable of functioning.

Key Terms

allocution
blaming the victim
crime victim
individualized guilt
Lifestyle-Exposure Theory
restitution
retaliation
Routine Activities Theory
self-protection
social control from below
universal human rights
victim impact statement (VIS)
victim self-help
victim-precipitated crime
victimology
Victims of Crime Act of 1984 (VOCA)
victims' bill of rights
Victims' movement

Questions for Study

1.   What are some of the costs of crime for victims?

2.   What does it mean to say that crime victims are twice victimized?

3.   What is the victims' movement, and how has it changed the situation of victims of crime?

4.   How does the risk of becoming a crime victim vary by age, race, and sex?

5.   What do lifestyle-exposure theory and routine activities theory imply about ways that victimization can be reduced?

6.   Is some crime victim-precipitated, or is this idea just an example of blaming the victim?

7.   What are some of the rights that victims possess at each stage of the criminal justice process, from the initial reporting of the incident, to execution of the offender?

8.   What programs that have been developed to allow crime victims to recoup monetary losses?

9.   In what ways do victims and potential victims sometimes act on their own behalf--without relying on criminal justice agencies--to protect themselves and to retaliate against offenders? How might victim self-help be viewed by the consensus and conflict perspectives?

Selected Readings

Julie A. Allison and Lawrence S. Wrightsman, <u>Rape: The Misunderstood Crime</u> (Newbury Park, CA: Sage, 1993). A broad analysis of rape, with particular focus on victims.

Dorothy Ayers Counts, Judith K. Brown, and Jacquelyn C. Campbell, eds., <u>Sanctions and Sanctuary: Cultural Perspectives of the Beating of Wives</u> (Boulder, CO: Westview Press, 1992). A collection of ethnographic case studies of violence in various settings across the world, from aboriginal Australia to desert Africa to modern Taiwan.

Robert Elias, <u>Victims Still: The Political Manipulation of Crime Victims</u> (Newbury Park, CA: Sage, 1993). Elias examines the ways in which crime victims and the victims' movement have been used to further the political agendas of conservative government crime control advocates.

Andrew Karmen, <u>Crime Victims: An Introduction to Victimology</u>, 3rd ed. (Belmont, CA: Wadsworth, 1996). A brief but comprehensive review of theory and research on victims of crime.

Charles J. Sykes, <u>A Nation of Victims: The Decay of the American Character</u> (New York: St. Martin's Press, 1992). Sykes argues that American culture has gone overboard in embracing the idea of victims.

Elie Wiesel, <u>Night</u> (New York: Bantam, 1982. Originally published by Hill and Wang, 1960). The Nazi's nearly-successful attempt to exterminate the Jews of Europe constitutes one of history's most unspeakable programs of victimization. In this short but powerful book, Elie Wiesel tells of his abduction as a boy and his experiences in the Nazi death camp at Auschwitz. Wiesel received the Nobel Peace Prize in 1986

Sample Test Questions

Multiple Choice Questions

1. Victims' expression of opinions in court in a personal, face-to-face appearance, usually during the sentencing phase of the offender's trial, is called _____.
    a. presentation
    b. allocution
    c. a victim impact statement
    d. citizen's inquiry

2. _____ refers to situations where the actions of persons lead directly to their becoming the victim of a crime.
    a. blaming the victim
    b. victim-precipitated crime
    c. common sense
    d. victimization likelihood activities

3. Measures that people take to protect themselves from becoming a victim, to defend themselves during a crime, or to punish offenders after the incident has occurred are referred to as _____.
    a. the crime clock
    b. victim-precipitated crime
    c. a victim-impact statement
    d. victim self-help

4. According to the text, international human rights efforts may be viewed as a type of _____.
    a. international victims' movement
    b. socialist propaganda
    c. international-level political manipulation of victims
    d. false consciousness

5. Routine activities theory suggests that people's likelihood of victimization is increased if _____.
    a. they present a suitable target for crime
    b. a potential criminal offender is present
    c. there is a lack of someone to prevent the incident
    d. (all of the above)

6. Lifestyle/Exposure theory suggests that people's likelihood of victimization is increased if _____.
   a. they encounter high-risk persons
   b. they enter high-risk places
   c. they enter certain areas during high-risk times of day
   d. (all of the above)

7. Andrew Karmen refers to restitution as a _____.
   a. sinking ship
   b. crumbling building
   c. city slum
   d. leaky net

8. In _____, the Supreme Court ruled that laws which limit criminals profits are unconstitutional.
   a. *Cooper v. Pate*
   b. *Simon and Schuster v. Members of the New York State Crime Victims Board*
   c. *Hudson v. Palmer*
   d. *Powell v. Alabama*

9. Research suggests that victim impact statements or allocution has what effect on judges' sentencing decisions?
   a. no demonstrable effect
   b. a small but significant effect
   c. a large effect
   d. a very large effect

10. By 1993, _____ states had passed legislation allowing victims to attend parole hearings.
    a. 24
    b. 30
    c. 43
    d. 50

True/False Questions

T F 11. The primary goal of criminal justice is prosecuting offenders, not satisfying victims of crime.

T F 12. According to the text, the direct monetary costs of crime add up to a "yearly crime tax" of about $425 for each U.S. citizen.

T F 13. According to Robert Elias, government victims policy has embraced conservative groups while systematically excluding those holding more liberal and critical viewpoints.

T F 14. According to the NCVS, the group that is most likely to be victimized by crime is the elderly.

T F 15. Lifestyle/exposure theory suggests that victimization is unrelated to where the criminal act occurs, who the victim is, or at what time of day the act happens.

Essay Questions

16. Discuss the role that crime victims play in the criminal justice process. What rights do victims have, if any?

17. Discuss the contributions made by the victims' movement. On what grounds has the victims movement been criticized?

18. Which persons and groups are most likely to become a victim of crime in the United States? How is victimization related to the availability and use of firearms?

19. Several theories have been proposed to explain victimization. Discuss these theories, and what they imply about how to reduce levels of victimization.

20. What programs are available through which crime victims can seek repayment of some of their monetary losses? How effective are these programs?

Answers to Sample Test Questions

1b, 2b, 3d, 4a, 5d, 6d, 7d, 8b, 9a, 10c, 11T, 12T, 13T, 14F, 15F